HOW TO WRITE AND SELL
A SYNOPSIS

HOW TO WRITE AND SELL A SYNOPSIS

Stella Whitelaw

ALLISON & BUSBY

First published in 1993 by
Allison & Busby
an imprint of Wilson and Day Ltd
5 The Lodge
Richmond Way
London W12 8LW

ISBN 0 7490 0150 X

Typeset by TW Typesetting, Plymouth, Devon
Printed and bound in Great Britain by
Mackays of Chatham Ltd, Lordswood, Chatham, Kent

CONTENTS

1

INTRODUCTION

Would you like a new friend? I know I would. An introduction is how one starts getting to know a new friend, so you can look upon this chapter as the beginning of a friendship. You, me and the communication of words and thoughts . . . in one word, writing.

Once I longed for a book like this to read. I needed it desperately, a beginner writer struggling in a jungle of half-formed, half-heard words of advice. Colour me lost.

Even now I'd far rather be reading this book than writing it. I am addicted to 'how-to' books about writing. It's as if by buying the book, one suddenly assumes the mantle of success without all the work . . . The same wishful thinking that goes with buying a size twelve dress when you need to shed half a stone.

The 'how-to' book acts as a carrot, the same way as that unworn size twelve dress will goad you into dieting. The book is your guide and encouragement, your friend in need. Every writer was once a beginner, and even after publication, we begin afresh with each new book.

It's so easy to give in; not to try any more. A mug of 40-calorie hot chocolate by my side, several cats on my lap, a good book to read and you can keep those long hours of night-owling at a typewriter.

But does this make a writer? No, this makes a lotus-eater.

There is one word that describes the truly professional writer: obsession. The obsession with writing and keeping on writing whatever the hiccups, the let-downs, the rejections.

Obsession comes in different forms. It means thinking like a writer all the time. Even a night out at a party can be termed research. All those people, faces, clothes, impressions . . . new stories popping into mind . . . overheard conversation . . . Nothing is wasted. The mental filing cabinet is rattling away, storing scraps of information.

Research is only one part of the writing obsession. Making notes, talking to people, seeing new places – villages, castles, rivers – taking an interest in everything . . . obsession is when you never stop being a writer.

Let's start the introductions. My name is on the front cover, which saves repeating it, and that's my real name. I am a writer and I am obsessed by writing. No day is complete without writing, be it on a typewriter, keyboard, or in longhand. The pen is not yet obsolete. A day without a single word written is a day wasted which I can never recover from passing time. My idea of hell would be if Lucifer handed me a typewriter but said they were clean out of paper.

I started writing seriously at the age of nine. I published, single-handed (editor, writer, illustrator) a weekly magazine with stories, serials, puzzles and competitions. As I was going through a religious phase, all the blank spaces were filled in with prayers. I sold this little magazine at a penny a copy. Without even going on a Youth Training Scheme, it dawned on me that I would save myself a lot of laborious copying if I rented out the magazine at half-penny a time. My income doubled overnight.

I also wrote stories instead of paying attention in class (my arm cupped over the paper); wrote a long novel at the kitchen table instead of doing homework or studying for exams; scribbled in bed under the sheets instead of getting my growing sleep. No wonder my parents despaired of me. Still I made 5 ft 6 ins and scraped through the exams.

I became a cub reporter on a South London newspaper in the hope of learning how to write. My chief reporter, Vic Davies (*Daily Sketch*, *Daily Express*, *Mail on Sunday*), taught me to use short words and preached humility as he tore my stories into shreds and fell about laughing. I survived this hard apprenticeship and became one of the first women chief reporters and certainly the youngest. I began to get short stories published in women's magazines and then, to my amazement, books were published. Running totals to date are over 180 short stories published and 25 books. I've lost count of the foreign or large-print sales. They are the icing on the cake.

Now it's your turn to introduce yourself, please. I'd like to get to know you. You could be 15, 35 or an active, zany going-on-70. Who wants to see a birth certificate? Tear it up – forget it. There's no set age for writing. Writers don't grow old, they only mellow.

You may be in one of these groups:

- A complete beginner. Not merely green round the ears but a total skin coverage.
- A writer with a few isolated successes and an aching ambition to achieve more.
- A moderately successful author who cannot resist reading 'how-to' books.

If you are an extremely successful author, a household and television name with the luxury of a secretary, then maybe you'll send him or her out to buy this book for your friends. But you won't need to read it, for you'll know how to structure a synopsis, plot an outline and polish your final words.

Hold on a minute, my lion-like flame-haired Persian wants to go out. Notice how easily I am diverted? Now a tortoiseshell

Persian wants to come in. The rescued family of nursing mother and three scallywag kittens can't make up their minds. Am I really prepared for a life-time role of doorman? No, it's time to work.

The spark

Writers are always debating the chicken and egg situation: which comes first, the plot or the characters? What starts a story off? There is no rust-solid rule, no golden ratio. There are no rules in writing at all – except the big three which shall never be mentioned in this book ... well hardly ever. They should be as natural as breathing:

- Double spacing.
- Clean presentation.
- Return postage.

Once said, never to be repeated, I hope. But they are so often forgotten. And I, as a professional writer, cannot understand why. It's like forgetting how to type.

Every writer varies in their method of beginning a new piece of writing. We each have a different moment of conception. Some say they always start with a character or group of characters and the story comes naturally from them; others begin with a plot or setting that they particularly want to use.

My stories have had different conceptions. I don't conform. Nothing is ever the same. Some came from a beginning, some from an ending; some from people, a line of dialogue, an interesting place, something that fascinated me or sent my mind spinning. I don't stop to think what starts off a story –

once in hand it's not important – but very soon the characters take over. They have to be strong or a story will not come to life.

My head is steaming full of characters, all seeking existence. Sometimes when I have finished a story, the clamour is unbearable. 'Me next!' 'Me next!' they shout, knocking at the door of my brain, kicking down the drawbridge. No patience. Unmannered lot.

Revision

Some people think they have only to write the required number of words, be it 50,000–70,000 words for a book, or perhaps a 1,500-word coffee break, mini-mystery, or 2,000-word short story and that's that. It is a book. It is a short story. But that is not that. It's merely the beginning. Now comes the hours of revision, rewriting and polishing until every word is like a diamond, honed to perfection.

I can agonise for days over one word, knowing the one I have chosen is not quite right. Eventually I may hand it to my unconscious (read Dorothy Brande's *Becoming a Writer*) and hope the answer will come into my head, probably when I'm least expecting it and when I can't write it down. Odd words and lines of dialogue often arrive when I'm swimming my twice-weekly half-mile. (A fortune awaits the inventor of waterproof paper.)

I even started writing this book whilst in the bath, elbow deep in moisturising foam. Soggy notes decorated the bathroom tiles till they fell off. It's no use vowing to write it all down later. You'll forget. Those priceless words will be lost forever in foam, traffic jams or Sainsbury's check-out queue.

What will this book be about?

Planning

So this book is going to be about planning – that is, sorting a book out in your mind, deciding on its theme, assembling conflicts and dramatic scenes into a form called a synopsis. You may think you don't need to bother about a synopsis; you'll just get on and write the book. Very commendable and it's one way of working, but sooner or later, and we all hope it's sooner, you are going to need to send your editor a synopsis and first three chapters.

And a synopsis is invaluable as a personal reference map. Don't be put off. Learn how to write a synopsis. Twelve easy steps, I promise you. Like going back to school or baking a cake.

Plotting

Plotting your story in detail can be fun, although at first it may feel an impossible task. All those accusingly empty rectangles waiting to be filled in. But it'll look so professional on the wall by your desk. Impresses the family, neighbours, the vicar.

It's like a game of chess, moving characters and scenes around, pencilling in a graph of emotion and drama, highlights and troughs of despair. Again you may think you don't need a sheet of cardboard on your wall (the board from all that shirt packaging is ideal), but it's certainly the quickest way of getting straight back to work, on course for the storyline, on a day when ideas are low and inspiration nil.

Polishing

Polishing is my favourite part of writing. The bliss of just concentrating on the arrangement of one sentence at a time. No worrying about what's going to happen next. You've done all that, the slog of getting the first draft down on paper is over. All those words exist.

You are entitled to congratulate yourself on your industry. Now comes the polishing, which is hard work of a different colour. This is the absorbing pleasure of making sure every word is in its correct place, that each word says exactly what you want it to say . . . a sentence at a time. Every unnecessary word is removed. Your writing is purged of excesses, made pure, made clean. Adjectives and adverbs are eliminated. It's cleansing and invigorating. Revise and revise. Hone, sharpen, whittle, polish. This is your chance to add poetry, paint pictures.

Writers' jargon

The technical terms used by writers, such as 'voice', 'style' and 'back-story', may puzzle many beginners. Sometimes they puzzle me too because I've been writing for years without consciously thinking about them. Yet we need to know exactly what they mean. A new writer told me recently that these terms were like a foreign language. It made writing so complicated. He did not know what they meant.

'People keep talking about show and tell, but I don't understand. Show and tell what? Tell me the difference. Show me the difference. And what is voice? Whose voice?' he asked, bewildered.

I will explain the meanings of FIFTY WORDS EVERY WRITER NEEDS TO KNOW in a glossary and give examples.

Writer's block

How I feel for writers facing writer's block! Let's take it out of the closet. Perhaps we can help each other.

There are three kinds of writer's block, one of which is horrendous – the writer's nightmare when, after some personal trauma, you feel certain you will never write again. Life has suddenly emptied like a dried-up well. Perhaps you won't write, not for a long time.

The second kind is the temporary block on a story which was going well and suddenly comes to halt. No ideas. Hopeless. You want to chuck it all in a bin and go for a long walk, preferably round the Isle of Dogs.

The third is self-inflicted, the average writer's everyday reticence to start work whatever the time.

It's a constant battle. Cats, coffee, reading old newspapers, gazing out of the window . . . they are everyday time-wasters. The world outside seems far more fascinating. I know I could write about it if only I had the time . . . and after I've washed the kitchen floor. Look at all those people, cars, clouds, clowns . . . I shy away from the commitment to work, the discipline, knowing that once I am hooked, I won't be able to stop and nothing will drag me away. What meals? Are people starving? Who wants to eat anyway? I can live on Bombay Mix. I can even dig out the lentil bits from the keyboard with a bent paperclip.

Writer's block, all three kinds, can happen to any of us, any time. It might help to be a little more prepared, not to despair, to try ways of lifting the weight.

Last Friday I saw an owl in my headlights, sitting in a puddle by the side of the road. He was having a shower, splashing about. He was big and splendid, speckled, black-eyed, utterly fearless. I was speechless with wonder. The sight of this owl, so close, so trusting, a creature from the wild, was captivating. He was in my territory – or was I in his? Whatever the answer, our encounter was a gift.

One day I may write a story about that owl. I've no idea what it will be about, but the image of that wild creature is stored in my mind, and so is the feeling. That owl will be a spark.

This book is also about sparks. The golden rain of thought that glows in the darkness and which writers reach out to catch with eager hands.

The next chapter is about the **synopsis**. Writing a good synopsis may be the means of selling your book.

2

THE DREADED SYNOPSIS

Synopsis is a peculiar word. It sounds like an illness, something vaguely septic, and the mention of it frequently brings on symptoms of despair and wretchedness in writers. My dictionary says:

SYNOPSIS – a condensation or brief review of a subject, a summary.

If you think of *opsis* as meaning a *view*, then the word is not nearly so alarming. The prefix *syn* means *with*, *together* or a *fusion*. A fusion of a view is pleasant, even poetic. Your fusion of your view makes it personal to your story. If *Roget's Thesaurus* is permanently in your right hand, then you will already know that he gives three further meanings:

- arrangement
- list
- compendium

Aim to remember

- Your synopsis must be stunning and professional.

11

- The time and care spent on it will bring its own reward.
- The writing of your synopsis should be of equal worth to the writing of your whole book.

Still you may ask: what is a synopsis? A synopsis shows the contents and flavour of a novel in a brief form. It sounds simple but it isn't. To produce a good synopsis is hard work. It could be compared to a very short narrative story.

Why is it important? Because if you don't know what your book is about, how will an editor be able to tell if they could sell it or you can write it?

Why is it important to get it right? A poor synopsis will sabotage your novel before it even gets off your screen. Every embryonic idea deserves a good start even if it flounders along the way.

By now the thought of beginning a synopsis should be less alarming. By making it workable, almost human, taming the dragon, it need no longer be one of the chores that writers put off doing. (The other chore is tax returns.)

There are three basic functions of a synopsis:

- The first is as a visible aid for the writer.
- The second is to attract the interest of an editor in your work.
- And, thirdly, eventually to sell your book.

Your own personal *opsis*

This amazing story idea that you have germinating and growing in your mind needs sorting out into some sort of order before you start writing, and a synopsis is one way to do it. You must have a clear idea what your book is about and where it is going to go. This helps you decide whether you really do have a story and whether there is enough plot to fill the required number of pages, fixes its identity and sets the boundaries. It's no good waffling about with a story that spreads aimlessly all over the place, out of control.

First write everything down that comes into your mind about this new story . . . scenes, high points and lows, bits of dialogue, characters . . . all the odds and ends, a fictional jumble sale. You could be organised and use a notebook. You could be hopeless and scribble on old envelopes. It simply doesn't matter. But get everything down that you know about your novel and put it all in one place . . . a file, a cereal box, the cat's basket, anywhere as long as you know where it is.

Authors are allowed to be eccentric. But it won't work if your novel is strewn like confetti all over the house and you spend precious hours searching for one vital piece of paper.

Your synopsis is a sales pitch, your commercial. You have got so many minutes, so many lines in which to sell your book. Make every minute of an editor's reading time work for you.

A synopsis is quite different from an outline, which is a more detailed, chapter-by-chapter blueprint that charts the progress of a plot, graphs the highs and lows, reminds you of easily forgotten sub-plots and loose ends. An outline is your day-to-day work manual, your own personal route map.

The synopsis and an outline are often confused. A synopsis is written in narrative form; an outline is a chart showing the progress of your plot. You would not send a progress chart to an editor – this is your own visual prop and guide. But you will refer to your synopsis – and often – to remind yourself of the main thrust of your story.

At the same time, there is no rule that says you have to keep to your synopsis. It isn't cast in concrete. It isn't a straitjacket. If, much later, you or your characters dictate a different twist or turn, then follow it. This is fine as long as the main theme stays the same and the leading characters still hold the floor. A contemporary romance that suddenly turns into science fiction or gothic horror has lost its identity; a minor character that takes over and ousts the hero has to be brought under control.

Attracting an editor's attention

The prime reason for writing a synopsis is to attract an editor's attention. In these days, the slush piles of unsolicited and hopeless manuscripts are enough to send overworked editors jumping off Kings Reach Tower or Richmond Bridge. It makes sense to send in a partial, something less than a complete manuscript. No writer wants to run the risk of wasted time and effort, or adding to an editor's heavy workload.

A partial consists of the first three chapters, a synopsis and a brief letter of personal introduction. The synopsis tells an editor several things about you and your book:

- whether you have a story there
- whether the story is different, unique, or has some special quality
- whether you know what you are doing and where you are going
- whether you can sustain the story and if there is enough plot for the proposed length
- whether the novel slots into one of their categories
- whether they have already published something similar

The three sample chapters show the editor that you can put the story together in an easy, readable style.

An editor does not need the complete manuscript of your

novel in order to assess these points. At this stage, though, an editor can make helpful suggestions, spot weaknesses, guide your work towards publication.

Listen to any suggestions from an editor and be receptive. An editor's interest is valuable, and any advice is worth thinking about even if you do not agree or follow it to the letter.

This gives an editor a chance to say if the plot is a bit thin, if she likes the characters, if there are too many, if a major scene in a butcher's shop is not suitable however strongly you feel about red meat. She will also comment on the doom and gloom aspect of your story, whether there is sufficient content for an uplifting or satisfactory ending.

If an editor suggests changes, it is much less frustrating to do this before you have progressed too far into the book. Ignore such advice at your peril.

Unless you are really famous, editors do not commission fiction on the strength of a synopsis. But they can and do express an interest, and that's important and worth having. Non-fiction is the exception to this rule. A non-fiction work could be commissioned on a more detailed chapter-by-chapter synopsis, two sample chapters and known writing ability.

On a practical side, sending a partial saves a lot of money and the cost of sending a heavy manuscript, with return postage, can be a big outlay. ('Mummy, they liked your parcel,' my small daughter once said, relaying a telephone message.)

There are many writers who never work with a synopsis and would not dream of producing one. They say it kills the story for them. They have no clear track of where their story is going. They begin with an idea that grows along with their characters and takes on a life of its own. If this is the way you prefer to work, then go ahead. Do what works for you. I'm not a guru.

But don't expect much editorial advice or interest. They can't comment on a vague idea shrouded in a fictional mist.

Other writers prefer to finish the whole novel and then submit a partial with a synopsis. The problem with this method is that when the whole book is before you in all its cleanly typed glory, it can be difficult trying to decide which are the major scenes. You get side-tracked by the delicious little bits and pieces that you cannot resist including in the synopsis to show editors how clever you have been.

Tense and timing

A synopsis is written in the present tense. The past tense is used for any references to past history. And when you have sent off your partial, don't sit back and think, oh good, now I can have a month off, go fishing. Carry on writing. Don't stop the creative flow. If you wait - possibly six weeks - for a reply, it might be hard work getting back into your story.

If the editor wants drastic changes, all is not lost. Some of the work that you have done in that waiting period can be salvaged and your characters will still be very much alive in your mind. The important thing is that your story has not gone cold on you, and if you have to jettison a few weeks' work, it has to be done. Log it as writing practice and don't waste time mourning.

Length

Irving Wallace's synopsis for his book *The Prize* was 40 pages long. *The Prize* is a very complicated book. I suggest as a rough guide that one page of synopsis is about right for every 10,000 words of planned novel. So a five-page synopsis should cover a 50,000-word novel. Again, there are no rules, but make your synopsis shorter rather than longer.

I always used to hate writing synopses, and the obvious result was that I wrote dreadful ones. They were pathetic. I simply did not know what to put in them and paddled aimlessly around in circles, padding out the prose with any old rubbish. No wonder they were sent back. Here is an exaggerated example of a synopsis that doesn't work.

A pathetic synopsis

This story (no title mentioned) is about a man and a woman (no names) who meet on the fabulous cosmopolitan (jargon) ski-slopes of Austria (at least the setting is stated). Wonderful background of sparkling snow, parties, etc. (what does etc. mean?). I have not decided what they do for a living (really?) but of course the hero is very wealthy (how come?). They fall in love (when?) but he has a former girlfriend (oh, yes), a blue-eyed blonde bombshell (cliché) who makes a lot of trouble (what sort?) and the heroine gets very upset (how much?) about all this and rushes home to England in tears. All is lost and it becomes a hopeless patchwork of despair (padding). Eventually (how long?) they meet again (where?) and soon realise that they love each other madly (what makes them so sure?) and there is a happy ever after ending (what kind of happy ending?).

Nothing will happen from this synopsis. No editor is immediately going to reach for the phone. The author has little idea of what the story is about, does not know the characters, and I doubt if anyone will want to read it.

When I began to write for Mills & Boon, I found it was essential to submit a good synopsis with each new story idea put forward. I had to learn how to do it professionally if I wanted my editor to be interested in my next book. A synopsis is a sales tool. It has selling power. If I wanted to sell my next book, then it was up to me to produce a synopsis that was concise, bright, intriguing and of the highest possible writing standard.

I was determined to learn how to do it. Make-or-break time was staring at me from the screen.

Several weeks and toss-and-turn nights later, I had broken down the requirements of an average fictional synopsis into sixteen steps, the last four being optional. These four are my extras which I like to put in. They are my individual touches – but you are welcome to use them, or think up some new ingredients of your own. It's like baking a cake. And here is the recipe:

The step-by-step synopsis

1. The setting and title. Where and when the action takes place. This is one straightforward sentence saying where the story is set and when in time.

2. The hero and heroine or main characters. Introduce your main characters by name, age, professional background, making them sound special and alive. And any minor character who has an important role in the plot merits a tiny cameo. A couple of paragraphs is enough.

3. Add a few details of family background, wealth, status, history. One concise paragraph should be adequate.

4. The main critical situation at the opening of your novel. Briefly describe the thrust of your story in a single sentence.

5. Now the mood and tone of the piece. Try to create the atmosphere of your story in one sentence.

6. That special ingredient. If your story has something special or unique about it, say so in another sentence. And keep plugging the title.

7. The conflict and drama of the story. Get your teeth into this one but keep it to one strong and powerful paragraph. Quality writing always.

I expect you have realised by now that these *seven* points are the foundation of your novel and most of them will be the substance of your initial two chapters.

So, you may ask: why put this information in the synopsis if most of it is contained in the first two chapters? Answer: an editor gets the feel of the whole book from the synopsis; the sample chapters demonstrate your ability to follow a synopsis. She'll spot immediately if they don't tally and you have gone wildly off course. The first two chapters of a crime or thriller novel need an extra dimension. They have to intrigue, hint at what is to come, set the crime scene, introduce the sleuth, murderer or the victim, establish the forward-moving problem or mystery.

8. Major scenes. Mention the title again. This is the time to list several of the most important scenes – not every scene in the book, but tasters of what the reader can expect to enjoy. A bit like programme notes for an evening's television. Two paragraphs will do justice to this step.

9. The forwards and backwards movement of the story as endured by the characters. What are the ups and downs, the positive and the negative side of the drama? And especially that darkest moment and how the main character is affected –

an emotional route-map in a single paragraph. Quite a tall order.

10. The decision-making scene. Now we are nearing the end. What is the scene that changes everything? It is crucial that the turning point is clearly signposted in a sentence.

11. The important final scene. The climax. The finale. A crescendo of invention in a dramatic paragraph.

12. A brief conclusion. Wrap it up in a good, satisfying sentence.

How long?

These twelve steps will tell an editor everything she needs to know about your story. (Seventy per cent of publishing staff are female.) It will also tell her a lot about you, so it pays to take trouble and to write it to the very best of your ability. Don't worry if steps 5 and 9 are too difficult to summarise. They are difficult. If in doubt, leave out.

It is generally thought that a synopsis should be one page long for each proposed 10,000 words of novel. So a synopsis for a 70,000-word novel would be seven pages long. But Mills & Boon, whose books are 50–55,000 words long, prefer a shorter synopsis and ask for two to three pages at the most. A short synopsis is better than one that goes on forever, provided that every necessary step is covered. Think of that tired editor wading through endless pages of typescript and give her a break.

And no secrets please. The editor will not be amused if you hint coyly that there is a brilliant twist ending, but you aren't going to tell anyone yet. By all means save small surprises to amaze your editor when she reads the complete manuscript, but the end of the story should be clearly stated in your synopsis. Okay, the butler did it. Trust her, the editor won't tell a soul.

Lastly use strong words, strong verbs. Make everything

exciting and dramatic. Even that pathetic synopsis had the name-less heroine *rushing* home to England, not merely travelling.

The optional four

13. A single line of dialogue from the heroine or main character. I like including this. They should be words which really show her character and style and the way she talks. Make it vivid. You've only got this one chance.

14. Example of dialogue from the hero or another character. This should also show his character and make him come striding off the paper. Let the editor hear his voice, preferably with a line that is pertinent to the plot.

15. Example of emotional or sensuous writing if this is relevant to your story. Show that you can write something really romantic, full of emotion. Or something electrifyingly chilling and exciting if it's a thriller. Again this is a taster, showing off your writing skill.

16. Putting in the poetry, painting a picture. This is a chance to add – only a few words, please, a single phrase at the most – something visual and poetic that gives your synopsis that extra dimension. Be on that moorland, smell that sea, hear those birds. Add a brush of poetry.

These four steps can be put into your synopsis at any point, wherever it seems most natural. You might add an example of dialogue after step 4 (main critical situation) and another after step 7 (conflict and drama). An example of emotional or sensuous writing might fit in after your paragraph of major scenes. As for that touch of poetry, the rainbow chasing your mind . . . it can go in anywhere.

* * *

Peter Mark Roget was an English physician who wrote his *Thesaurus of English Words and Phrases* in 1852 when he was retired. He was already 73 years old and lived another seventeen years. When I reach that great writers' conference in the sky, I hope to meet him. I should like to thank him for producing this invaluable writers' bible. When I recorded the programme *Desert Islands Discs* in the Falklands, *Roget* was my choice of book to take along to that treeless sweep of mined and booby-trapped white sand.

'Hello Dr Roget,' I'll say to him. 'It's a wonderful book. Did you have to submit a synopsis?'

'A synopsis?' he'll say thoughtfully. 'Arrangement, list, compendium? Graduation, classification, order, digest? Catalogue, inventory, schedule? Precis, analysis, summary?'

'In a nutshell, Peter,' I'll agree. 'In a nutshell.'

3

LET'S WRITE A SYNOPSIS

By now you may feel confident enough to try writing a synopsis of your own. This is best written in longhand first on a big pad of paper with plenty of room allowed for alterations and additions. Rule off a left-hand margin and at intervals put a word or two that will remind you of the sixteen suggested steps.

The reminders could be: 1. SETTING, 2. MAIN CHARACTERS, 3. BACKGROUND, 4. CRITICAL SITUATION, 5. MOOD, 6. SPECIAL INGREDIENT, 7. CONFLICT, 8. MAJOR SCENES, 9. UPS AND DOWNS, 10. DECISION, 11. FINALE, 12. CONCLUSION plus 13. DIALOGUE (f), 14. DIALOGUE (m), 15. SENSUALITY, and 16. POETRY.

Work slowly and methodically, one paragraph at a time. Simplify and condense the storyline. Tighten every sentence.

When you come to type it up (double-spacing, of course, and a decent black ribbon) begin with a heading that gives relevant information. Also put your address at the top of the first page and the expected length of the novel. Like this:

Your address

THE TITLE
Planned length, say: 70,000 words/10 chapters
a romance/thriller/murder mystery (whatever)
by
Your writing name

Then start typing your synopsis, set out in normal paragraphs in double-spacing. No need to invent a fancy layout.

A sample synopsis

This is the final synopsis of my book called *Daughter of Tor*, showing how I used the sixteen steps to give the clearest possible analysis of the plot. It went through three drafts before it was ready to send off.

My address

DAUGHTER OF TOR
10 chapters/50–55,000 words
a romance
by
Stella Whitelaw

Synopsis

1. This modern-day romance erupts during a scorching summer term at Belling Hills, an expensive girls' boarding school in South Devon, near Dartmoor and the beautiful South Devon coast.

[Note deliberate use of verb 'erupt'; also I have stated the duration of the story as being three months of a summer term. Even the weather is mentioned.]

2. Sister Troy Kingsbury is the resident sister at the school's medical centre, a tall, sensitive woman in her late twenties, recovering from a traumatic divorce and needing to find herself a new identity. The headmistress, Grace Howard, has a brother,

Jonathan Howard, who at 36 sees his career as an orthopaedic surgeon virtually at an end.

[Thumbnail sketches. Note: there's very little about appearance; not necessary at this stage unless it is crucial to story, i.e. someone is blind. The hardest character to write about is a deaf person. Think about it.]

3.   The repossession of her married home caused Troy severe anguish after her divorce. Living in the Coastguard's Cottage on the school estate is helping to restore her confidence when Jonathan arrives to convalesce after a helicopter accident in which the nerves of his hands have been severed, and his confidence destroyed.

[Note: no long rigmarole. Plain facts stated, using strong words.]

4.   The conflict arises from Troy's indignation and distress at being turned out of her beloved cottage for a man, a top medical man who gives every indication that he's about to interfere with the way she runs the medical centre too.

[Note: this gives strong clues about their characters . . . Troy's distrust of men; Jonathan's natural arrogance.]

5.   The tone of *Daughter of Tor* is the paradox of raging calm; their raging and passionate emotions against the calming background of sea, hills and cliffs, with nature reflecting their changing moods.

[Note: I'm hoping this is going to work. As I haven't written it yet, my fingers are crossed. *Raging Calm* is an alternative title – there is no copyright in titles and it has been used before by Stan Barstow, but it's almost perfect.]

6.   Two emerging issues are the recognition of the subtle physical and emotional signs that could mean a child is being abused, and the importance of child bereavement therapy which is often ignored. These serious themes run through the whole story, giving it a backbone of strength and caring.

[Note: this says that the story is not only a complicated,

sensual romance . . . there are also important social issues.]

7. Troy has to fight Jonathan on several levels; his interference in her job, his apathy about ever being fit to operate,
and her growing attraction to him when she thought such
feelings had gone forever. They cross swords at every meeting,
their angry exchanges heightened by hidden emotions.

[Note: it would be wrong to detail all these small scenes even
if you are longing to share the exciting dialogue you have
already heard in your head. Write them down somewhere else.]

8. Major medical scenes include a girl pupil hit on the head
during games; a boy saved from drowning; a distressed
runaway and her forceful exam-mad parents; a pupil whose
mother dies unexpectedly; an asthmatic girl locking herself in
a lavatory to smoke and Jonathan climbing up to rescue her;
a local farmer seriously gored by a bull; life-saving surgery in
farm kitchen.

[Note: since this story has a medical background, the chief
medical scenes are detailed. An editor might say no to some
illnesses or operations, AIDS or abortion, for instance.]

The emotional tangle grows as Troy finds herself falling in
love with Jonathan, and the arrival of his awkward thirteen-
year-old daughter, Amanda, does nothing to help. Troy dis-
covers his wife left him years ago and has since died. He is
like another lost child for all his skill and reputation. She longs
to tell him that she cares, but he recoils from her tenderness,
believing he has nothing to offer her and that the wayward
Amanda is an even greater barrier.

[Note: new twist introduced, new character.]

9. When Troy and Jonathan are walking the spectacular South
Devon coastal path, or exploring the steeply stepped streets of
Dartmouth, they find much to enjoy in each other's company.
Troy tries to help him exercise his fingers – keyboard typing,
playing the piano. But the moment they get too close, Jonathan
backs off, leaving her humiliated that she has allowed her

emotions to show and her physical desire to be aroused. He tells her that he will never trust a woman again, that she should forget him; he has no intention of ever allowing another woman into his life.

Meanwhile the threads of the other storylines are woven into the romance: Troy becomes alerted to a girl's unconscious calls for help; the bereavement therapy shows positive results and the two girls, Lucy and Sarah, respond to Troy's warm-hearted attention, eventually becoming friends.

[Note: pulling the threads together.]

10. The scene which changes the situation is when Jonathan is forced to do an emergency operation on the gored farmer, who may die from loss of blood. With the return of his confidence and the mobility of his fingers, he realises that his career is all-important again, but hesitates to tell Troy, knowing it will make her unhappy. He returns abruptly to London, without even saying good-bye, leaving Troy desolate and heartbroken.

[Note: this is called the darkest moment.]

11. A freak autumn storm blows up; people are injured by falling trees and in fishing-boat accidents. Troy is too busy tending casualties at Loop Cove to think of her cottage, standing so close to the cliff's edge. But Jonathan drives down overnight from London, knowing she might be in danger, just as the garden of the Coastguard's Cottage disappears in a landslide. He saves her from death as the rear wall of the cottage plunges over the cliff.

[Note: be brief, be dramatic.]

12. They realise that they love each other and cannot live apart. They work out how this can be made possible, with a new life for Amanda and hope for the other two girls in the story.

[Note: tie up the loose ends quickly.]

* * *

The last four optional pieces can be inserted anywhere or omitted altogether. In your synopsis, you are the boss. I like to put them in, if it seems natural and adds texture to the synopsis. So, four more steps and it's done.

13.   'I hope you will recognise that I'm in charge of the medical health of these girls and I won't stand for any interference on your part,' says Troy. 'You may be a very important surgeon in London, but down here, you're just the man living uninvited in my cottage.'

[Note: you can hear her voice and she states the conflict situation again.]

14.   'Saved him? Yes, I suppose I did save the boy because I happen to be capable of blowing oxygen into his lungs. But what about those patients, young and old, who have little or no future beyond pain and immobility and all because of me, because of my hands?' Jonathan's face pales, his voice numb with anguish. 'What use is a surgeon who can't hold a knife steady?'

[Note: his voice is clear and his anguish over his injured hands apparent.]

15.   He takes her face in his hands, tracing her skin with gentle fingers, catching his breath sharply as she moves closer. Their mouths touch, tentatively at first, tasting a new, tantalising taste, both suddenly shaken by an impatience that catches them unawares. 'Who taught you to kiss like this?' he asks. 'You did,' she whispers.

[Note: just enough to show that you can write a tender love scene.]

16.   Bold and silent hills ... changing sea songs ... wind tangled skeins ... rags of clouds ... silken skin ... poppy bruised ... icepick thoughts ... daisies umbrellaed with dew ... sheared cliffs ...

[Note: a phrase, nothing more, somewhere.]

* * *

28

That's my synopsis for *Daughter of Tor*. [The paragraphs are numbered as a guide for you. Don't number your synopsis.] It's not *Gone with the Wind* but it does say a lot about *Daughter of Tor* and leaves me free to expand in any way that I want. I'm not tied to anything and I'm going to enjoy writing it. I can feel the scenes fairly leaping off the page. Sparkle and spontaneity can have their way. And they probably will.

As Michael Legat says in his book *Plotting the Novel* (Hale), 'Like most self-imposed disciplines, that of working to a synopsis becomes a freedom.' How true.

Don't be put off by the thought of the hard work that goes into writing a synopsis. It is going to save you time and trouble eventually. It becomes a friend at hand, and because you have done it, you are now free to write.

Katherine Anne Porter wrote: 'Courage is the first essential.' And Humpty Dumpty says: 'When it comes to words, it's a matter of who's to be master, that's all.'

4

THE OUTLINE

There is such confusion over the difference between a synopsis and an outline. Some publishers want a synopsis and some want an outline; other publishers want a chapter-by-chapter breakdown and call that a synopsis. Some want both. And the poor writer is somewhere in the middle hoping to provide what the publisher wants.

I work on the concept that a synopsis is a way of selling a book, like a detailed but pithy advertisement. The outline is the way the writer develops the plot for his or her own use: stepping-stones, a guide through the maze.

They are linked. The writer must remember to put into the outline all the important scenes and aspects described in the synopsis. The outline should follow the synopsis closely at first, but be prepared for it to change, like all living things.

So an outline is a chapter-by-chapter breakdown of your novel. F. Scott Fitzgerald's method was to have a separate sheet of paper for each chapter and pin them round the walls like washing. I prefer to use one large piece of cardboard – that from a shirt package is ideal – or a large sheet of paper. I want to be able to see the whole outline, the entire book in scenes at a glance. It gives me a sense of balance, a sense of purpose. I know where I'm going.

Why is an outline helpful?

A plot outline is a blueprint. It is your personal route-map that will take you from the opening paragraph to when, exhausted and parched, eventually you type the word END. It is a framework on which to plot the scenes in each chapter so that the action is well placed, to graph the high and low points in the story, to show you where to plant clues and red herrings. It reminds you when it's time to start winding up the story and tidy up the loose ends. Readers like a satisfactory ending. It may be clever to give all the answers on the very last page but it does leave the reader wanting something more substantial.

It is reassuring to know what you are doing and be able to scan the progress of the story on the outline. It also enables you to check whether the actions and motivations of characters stay within character.

Time spent on plotting an outline is time saved later. It could be your lifeline when you hit a barren patch. You may sit down at your desk ready to work after an unforeseen interruption, with your train of thought broken if not severed. Where were you in the story when you last worked? You read what you last wrote, revising and polishing as you read, of course. A word here, a word there. Every improvement helps. Your mind drags sluggishly across the page. You seem to have washed inspiration down the plug-hole when you last shampooed your hair.

But help is at hand. Your trusty outline. A glance at the plot for the current chapter and suddenly you know exactly what is the next move in the story, or the next scene, whether it's major or quite small. Write yourself in with a little narrative, some linking dialogue, even a few lines about the weather . . . and you are back in harness.

Starting to make an outline

Take the said large sheet of cardboard or paper, a ruler, pen or coloured felt tips if you are into coloured felt tips:

- Divide the sheet into equal sections according to the number of proposed chapters.
- Label each space Chapter 1, Chapter 2 etc. (Easy so far, isn't it?)

Now, before you go any further, re-read your own synopsis of the book. Note this account of your story and begin the mental pacing. Where exactly in the book is this scene going to happen, that confrontation take place?

- Briefly write in the details of the initial two chapters. You should sail through these two since you are already writing them.
- Take your time. Live with the idea, day in and day out. Don't let those precious ideas slip away like smoke signals. Have your outline at hand always, on your desk, by the telephone, next to the kettle, anywhere that's visible and accessible.

Now you can start playing with your coloured felt tips if you want to. Perhaps blue for background narrative, orange for major scenes, black for troughs of despair and red for the blushing roses of romance. It could work if your eyesight can stand the changing kaleidoscope for months on end.

My own system is less hi-tech. I prefer to use ordinary biro pens, some black, some blue. Important scenes are underlined. Major scenes are in capital letters. Love scenes are a square with L/S written inside (is this Freudian?). Some details are circled. There's also wavy underlining which means build on this. Question marks query items I'm not sure about.

You will soon develop your own graphics and shorthand. Fine, as long as you understand them and can remember what everything means weeks later. There's nothing more annoying than being confronted by something illegible with five exclamation marks and WOW! in caps.

- Write in major scenes, spaced out. A reader will soon lose interest if everything happens in Chapter 2 and then the story paddles along until another major scene blows up Chapter 10.
- Chart the highs and lows of emotion, conflict and drama, including the darkest moment. This kind of graph goes up and down like a temperature chart, the darkest moment coming at about two-thirds through. A rollercoaster ride with your heroine in the front seat.
- If romance figures strongly in your story, then it is sensible to make some decisions in advance. You certainly wouldn't plot every kiss, each hug, every tender moment. That would take away any romantic spontaneity – and we all crave plenty of r/s. But it does make sense to decide early on when your major love scenes will be and plot the setting, or you may find they take place in a broom cupboard or half way down the M1. Again, the reader will feel cheated if there are two love scenes in Chapter 3 and nothing more till a final breathless clinch on page 186.

    And where's the URST (Unresolved Sexual Tension)? Romances live on a diet of URST.
- Tie-ups and loose ends. There will be dozens of them and it does help to put in visual reminders.

How to change your outline

You can change your outline anytime. Feel free. A synopsis is not a contract which you dare not alter, nor is your outline tamper-proof. Characters often take over and change the direction of a story, or initiate better scenes than the ones you first thought of. So, it's okay to change things. Move them around.

Take a red pen and your ruler and draw neat arrows, not too big, discreet but bold. If a major scene plotted for Chapter 7 works better in Chapter 4, then arrow it straight to its new home. If Chapter 4 then overruns, move the unwritten scenes on to the next chapter – with smaller arrows.

You may then find that Chapter 7 is light without a major scene. Keep in mind that this needs replacing, but there's no need to rush in with a new subplot. You may find that if Chapter 4 has overrun, this is going to shift several scenes forward and the overrun of Chapter 6 will fill Chapter 7 very nicely.

Stories have a way of self-expanding, like popcorn heated in a pan. You may be in despair at the beginning with an outline that reads like a shopping list for one. But by the time you are halfway into your novel, you will have so much material you may have arrows going round to the back of the board.

Make your outline work for you. If it looks a mess, then it's alive and working. If nothing whatsoever has changed and all is clean and pristine, it's too good to be true. Find out if the patient is still breathing.

Scaffolding, symphonies and stakes

If preparing an outline totally eludes you, then perhaps you should ask yourself some honest questions and give yourself some honest answers. Perhaps you haven't really thought your story through.

Authors often see their novel projected in their minds like scenes on television, the cameras rolling, actors and actresses in place, almost word perfect. It's a conjuring trick that gets better with practice. It needs working on. I switch on when I'm swimming or walking; I carry my own personal, waterproof TV. If this is new to you and feels strange, then set aside a particular space in every day for thinking time, in the bath, waiting for a train, with your morning cuppa. This thinking time is invaluable.

Don't feel guilty about it. Thinking time is still working time. As Lord Ted Willis's family so kindly put it, 'Dad's writing in his head.'

Every line you write has invisible scaffolding. It's the thinking time before you put a word on paper. And the more scaffolding, the stronger your story.

Authors who never plan a synopsis or never plot an outline still go through a thinking process. They know their characters so well that they hardly need to wonder what is going to happen next. But, to strike a paradoxical note, a story is like a symphony. The instrumentalists are the ingredients of your novel and you are the conductor holding them together. But where would you be without a score? Everyone would be playing their own thing, in their own time, some might never get beyond tuning up. Imagine the chaos. My outline is my score.

So ask yourself some questions about this story you are going to write but don't know how to get started. Do I really care about this story? Have I got a theme? Is it a personal indulgence? What is this story about? What is at stake? And is this story going anywhere? Be honest. Don't try to write something that exists only in an unrealistic, airy-fairy way. People often say, don't they, 'Oh, I could write a fantastic book about what my father did in the war.' No, they couldn't. They just think they could. And I'm not simply talking about the dedication, the self-discipline, the hours of hard work that would be required. What they have in mind is not a professionally written piece of work but an indulgence. It is their conception of what a book is and the two things are not the same.

So **do you care** about this story? Are you obsessed with it? Are your thoughts constantly flying to it when you should be concentrating on other things, i.e. mundane work? Do you dream about it? Are the characters beginning to talk to you, give themselves names, likes and dislikes, occupations? Do you sit in front of the television and realise that you haven't taken in a single word? Do you passionately want to write this story? Do you feel that there will be a void in your life if you don't write it, that it's something you will always regret?

Do you really care **enough**? If your answers are all vaguely no, then sadly the story isn't for you. There must be this burning passion behind every piece of writing. I ache to write my short stories; they consume me with an intensity of longing to write them. I am passionate about writing this book. I want new writers to enjoy their writing, to be enthusiastic. I want to show them how I go about writing, to bombard them with useful hints.

A **theme** can be very simple. It doesn't have to be the stuff of an honours degree. It is the motivation behind the plot, an attitude. Rejection, insecurity, revenge, loneliness, loss of self-image, grieving, struggles, manipulation, hunger, mid-life crisis, finding oneself, hypocrisy, changelessness . . . it's the unifying idea that develops throughout a story. A person's need . . . the need to be loved, to belong, to be successful and many more.

There are endless themes. Read today's news stories and decide the underlying theme of each story. They will surprise you. To go back to that symphony score, the theme is the melody. (But you knew that.)

Self-indulgence is a deadly trap for the writer. There may be a personal story you're desperate to write because it satisfies some inner need. You've always wanted to write about how your interfering neighbours get their comeuppance, or your impossible boss suffers some horrible grisly end, or how you'd start a new political party and sweep to power in the polls in six and a half weeks. There may be a very big novel there, but are you quite sure that this fantasising isn't going to be just a bit boring for the reader? Write it by all means, if it gets these repressed feelings off your chest, but don't expect anyone else to read it.

That doesn't mean that the idea is no good. You need to distance yourself from it. If you take a personal experience, use that as a basis and develop it into a work of fiction. Don't write about your traumatic divorce. Let one of your characters go through a traumatic divorce. That firsthand knowledge will make it highly readable.

Sometimes a very personal story needs to be written as self-therapy. It works. I lost a baby and couldn't stop grieving. Then I wrote it out and the process seemed to go full circle.

So, **what's at stake?** If you don't know then there's a lot more thinking to do. Your characters are not living people yet. You have got to get to know them inside out, not just what makes them tick but what makes the tick tick.

Where the story is going is a verb. It becomes a non-plot when there is no movement and nothing much happens. If your story is static, it is not going anywhere. It hasn't any shape and is about as interesting as pink blancmange. A big yawn. It needs a fast injection of drama, conflict, of dynamic major scenes and a strong movement towards a satisfying conclusion. Think how boring the television programme *Casualty* would be if everyone had a headache.

And the reason for this movement goes back to **what's at stake**. A stake is a vertical post. Your story is fastened to this stake for support. No matter where the plot goes, the stake anchors it to reality and the reason for being there. Equally a stake is the valuable commodity that a player hazards on a gamble. It stays on the table while the competitors weave around in complicated manoeuvres. No stake, no story.

Timing

The outline gives you the opportunity to sort out the timing of your story. When exactly does it start and end? What are the seasons? How much time is covered? Signpost the passing of time. No point whatsoever in planning a dramatic scene in a snow blizzard if chronologically you're still in mid-September.

How old is everyone? Mark in that X is 23, Y 28 and Z 65. As time passes, keep a track of their increasing ages. In some books, babies have a funny way of remaining babies, or suddenly start attending school when barely walking.

It also surprises me how rarely characters have birthdays. Decide on your characters' birthdays and make them happen, even if in a low-key way . . . 'No one sent him a card.'

Historicals and sagas

The matching of a fictional/factual schedule is even more complicated if you are writing a book that spans a large or significant historical time period. You'll need more than one sheet of shirt cardboard. It helps to set out the fictional outline and historical facts side by side.

On the left-hand side of the allocated chapter space would go the fictional plotting, then on the right-hand side put the factual episodes, with dates, which you want to include or weave into the plot, wars, riots, fires, epidemics. These anchor the story to the historical turn of events at the correct time. And don't forget the changing reigns of kings and queens. Even a servant girl would hear about a king dying and a new one being crowned at Westminster.

Research

The same procedure should be followed for the linking of research items. Some authors go to immense trouble with their research, put all the information on to nice index cards, or file and number in clear-leafed folders; some even key their research on to a disc. Mark your outline with a relevant number reminding you where to find your filed or indexed piece of information e.g. 'Page 477 Peterloo massacre (Trevelyan)'.

Full marks if your research is so well organised.

I wish I could boast of some similar wonderful piece of penmanship. My organisation consists mainly of piles of paper on this table, on the carpet, on bookcases, on windowsills, going up the stairs. Don't touch, I know where everything is! And my excuse is lack of time.

I do have a system of sorts of using strips of paper to mark pages in books and writing on the top of the paper very clearly what that page contains and the number of the page. The page number is essential. Bits of paper have a habit of falling out every time you open a book and that page number can save hours of frantic re-reading.

However, for my next book I am resolved to use the clear-leafed folder system. Photocopy the page that contains the researched item, highlight the relevant part in yellow, pop into clear folder.

Crime and thrillers

Timing and research are crucial to the thriller or crime novel. The timing has got to be right. Dead right. It must be historically accurate even when the past is only yesterday. And the research about everything (guns, poisons, medical facts, ferry timetables, flight times, even bus routes) must be checked and double-checked, so you must know where you found the information in the first place.

Your red herrings and clues must be plotted in your outline, ready for planting in your story. I don't need to repeat how vital it is to get these right: a clue that is too early, or too late; a red herring that is never explained; the disguised clues that a reader might pick up later and think, 'how clever'.

It's a big puzzle and such fun to plot, especially if something ordinary you put in Chapter 2 suddenly has immense significance in Chapter 9. Your unconscious is at work.

Writers worry too much about plots. They panic. They think every possible story has already been written. This is a rumour put about by other worried writers. Every writer has a freshness, some new insight or twist to bring to a fairly ordinary or extraordinary situation. We are each a unique personality. No one else thinks quite the way you do, so use that uniqueness to create something different.

Invent, test, reject. Invent, test, save. Invent, pass, put in your outline. Soon you won't be able to wait to start writing. It'll be an itch you've got to scratch.

5

LET'S PLOT AN OUTLINE

This is shirt-cardboard time again. If you are inspired to write another sequel to *Gone with the Wind*, you'll need several sheets. For an average slim ten-chapter book, this size divides neatly into ten rectangular spaces, each about two-and-a-half by four inches.

Write the chapter number at the top of each space, then sit back and think things into an order.

What goes in first?

A story usually starts at a moment of change and this imaginary exercise is no exception. A mother's remarriage ... definitely a moment of change for any daughter. Then list all the other scenes in the same chapter, leaving plenty of room between the lines for adding points.

For example, the Chapter One box might read:

JANE LEARNS OF MOTHER'S REMARRIAGE
ANGRY PHONE CALL TO SISTER
ROW WITH MOTHER
JANE STALKS OUT OF HOUSE
CAR ACCIDENT

It's a sufficiently gripping opening chapter with plenty of drama and conflict, but hold on – there's lots more, isn't there? You know that when you write it, you'll be putting flesh on the bones. Chapter One is not simply those five scenes, one after another. You've planned to describe their interesting old house, Jane's demanding job, her broken love affair, her loss of confidence. More aspects to slot in, more characters to introduce.

So slot them in, using a different coloured pen, or lower-case (small) writing. The box for Chapter One might now look like:

JANE LEARNS OF MOTHER'S REMARRIAGE
    Broken love affair (flashback)
ANGRY PHONE CALL TO SISTER
    Jane's unhappiness/feelings/fear
    Describe sister
ROW WITH MOTHER
    Describe mother
    Description of Priory Manor
STALKS OUT OF HOUSE
    Jane's job (backstory)
CAR ACCIDENT
    Dramatic cliffhanger

Develop your own style of adding information. A personal shorthand is useful and saves space and long instructions. These are some of mine:

- Circle round name means character description
- Circle round place name means place description
- L/S in a square suggests a love scene
- Question mark means check this later
- Exclamation mark indicates high drama
- A large star [★] means 'note this' and may connect with other stars further on

- NAR means put narrative here
- MORE means exactly that – more . . .

There are all sorts of signs on your keyboard which could become writing shortforms. I'm longing to use # and § and the three styles of brackets ⟨ ⟩ { } and [ ], if only I could think of something they could stand for.

Look at the rest of Jane's story and where other major scenes might occur. Is the mother's wedding going to be in Chapter Three or Chapter Five? Write it in. If it's wrong, cross it out or draw a big arrow to its new place in the story. When does the sister turn up with Jane's ex-fiancé?

Don't put more than three major scenes in the same chapter (stalking out of the house cannot be classed as a major scene and the car accident, though dramatic, is not long enough to be regarded as a scene). Conversely, don't have one chapter with nothing at all happening. Spread major scenes around so that the whole book is progressively exciting. When is the new man in Jane's life going to turn up? Perhaps he's been there all the time and she didn't know? That could make an interesting twist.

Now let's leave Jane and her problems. I'm not going to write about them. Feel free if the storyline grabs you. But I am going to write a different adult story about children and two important childhood issues. The synopsis is ready (Chapter Three) and it's time to plot an outline.

Child abuse has been in the newspapers a lot recently and although I'm not going to go into sordid detail, I want to write about the latent signs. I also feel that little is done for the bereaved child; we tend to think they don't understand about death and don't bother with their feelings . . .

The outline for *Daughter of Tor*

This is going to be a little more complicated to plan because I have several threads of the story to weave along ... major scenes of conflict between my heroine and hero, Troy and Jonathan; the medical scenes; the unconscious signs in Lucy, the abused child; the bereavement therapy for sad Sarah. Four levels of plot as well as the romance ... no wonder I'm going to need an outline, for it could be all over the place. And, as it is a romance, it needs to be light reading with no heavy moralising, even though it deals with serious situations. Easy to get lost with so many things going on. I should definitely forget something important if I didn't have my blueprint, my route map, my trusty outline.

I can even start outlining backwards and sometimes it makes sense. It's reassuring to see that the end is strong and satisfying and you know where the story is going.

So straight to Chapter Ten with what I already know is going to happen:

FREAK AUTUMN STORM – trees/boats
TROY TENDS INJURED (What kind?)
JONATHAN DRIVES DOWN (fast)
TROY SAVING THINGS AS LANDSLIDE TAKES GARDEN
J SAVES HER
THEY CANNOT LIVE WITHOUT EACH OTHER L/S
AMANDA becomes BOARDER
LUCY and SARAH become FRIENDS

I'm not likely to get writer's block with all that going on. I may even think that I've got far too much for Chapter Ten and some of it – perhaps Lucy and Sarah becoming friends – would be better in Chapter Nine (big arrow), since they are subsidiary characters; Chapter Ten can then be devoted to my main characters.

Hold on, I'd forgotten all about Amanda, Jonathan's awkward thirteen-year-old daughter. Some creative re-scheduling is required. We'll have her arrive unexpectedly in Chapter Seven to give it a big lift. No, she should arrive either at the end of Chapter Six as a cliffhanger or the end of Chapter Seven. This decision to be made later. It'll come clear as I write on. Empty Chapter Eight could then be pretty emotional as Troy does not know, till then, that Jonathan has a daughter.

Next I'm going to plot in the medical scenes. We don't want too much blood and gore in the same chapter, but also there is the progression of some illnesses and medical-book references to put in. Patients don't disappear. The gored farmer has to be in Chapter Nine so that Jonathan can operate and find that his fingers are obeying all the right signals. The knocked-out-tooth incident is in Chapter One (I found this leaflet about knocked-out teeth at my dentist's – it made his bill worthwhile) and the drowning boy on the beach is definitely Chapter Two.

But enough talk . . . let's write them in. It'll make far more sense to you that way.

Let's have the Prince William re-run (hit on head during games) in Chapter Three (kept all the newspaper cuttings, of course), also progress of tooth at dentist's; the distressed runaways found on Dartmoor can go in Chapter Four. We'll have the scene with runaway's distraught parents in Chapter Five. Girl under exam pressure.

Young Sarah's mother dies at the end of Chapter Five and there is the school's reaction. And believe me, there is a reaction. Chapter Six sees Jonathan climbing up to the second floor to rescue an asthmatic girl who has locked herself in a lavatory to smoke. (Imagine Troy's distress, knowing his hands have little strength or feeling.)

The clues for Lucy will be plotted differently. Perhaps in

brackets (Lucy - headaches), with a new clue each chapter or so. I think I'll do the same for sad Sarah (Sarah - class behaviour).

The love scenes need to be thought about in advance. Although they must be spontaneous, it's far more romantic to have them taking cover from a rainstorm on Dartmoor rather than kiss while mopping up blood from colliding nose-bleeds. So plot them. One at about a third through, then perhaps another two-thirds through, approximately. That may sound manipulative and passionless but your characters will take over and the love scenes will come naturally. Such notes remind me to write them.

Sometimes I get so carried away with the story that I forget that the reader actually wants to read about my characters experiencing physical love. I know my characters well and I know it happens or has happened. But my readers want to read about it and share their emotions on the page. They will be disappointed if it is rushed or glossed over with the customary three dots . . . so love scenes in Chapter Four and Chapter Eight.

Chapter Eight is a bit empty, lots of white space staring at me. Poor old Chapter Eight could do with some romance. But don't worry, it won't be bleak for long. I know from experience that more ideas will occur as I begin to write.

And so it goes on. I'm building up an outline with all the information I have at the beginning. Chapter Eight is light, so what? I'm not too concerned . . . yet. Let's have them go to Dartmouth. It's such a lovely place, all those tinkling halyards and old stepped streets. But there must be a valid reason. I know as I go along that a reason will come into mind and new scenes will suggest themselves that were not in the synopsis. (What about that little inn overlooking the estuary at Dittisham? It had a marvellous view and was full of character . . . but not a meal . . . something different.)

Scenes can be added to the outline as I write. Ideas will come fast and in no time at all the chapters will be bursting with scenes and I'll be running out of space and length. There's no point in overwriting. I may have to cut some scenes out if they are not strong enough or do not contribute to the main story.

My cardboard outline is nearly full. By the end of writing the first draft of the novel it will look like a spider's web of crossed lines, bold notes in red, exclamation marks and boxes of tiny reminders.

Try plotting an outline for yourself. An easy way to practise is to make an outline of a book you have just finished reading. Scan each chapter and itemise its contents. But don't take too long over it. Your own writing is far more important. Plot an outline, even if you are half way through the first draft.

There's no pressure, no prizes. No one will see your outline and mark it out of ten.

Such fun.

But hard work. Writing is hard work. And I've said that before.

6

CREATING CHARACTERS

Characterisation is the prime ingredient of any book. Without characters there is no story, everything becomes sawdust. Even in this book there are two characters, you and me. You come over very strongly ... you exist as a person who wants to write, who is determined to write ... and I have a passion for writing.

The idea for *Daughter of Tor* has been swimming around in my mind for several weeks. It's not ready to write yet because there is still a lot to think about and sort out.

Thinking time

I cannot stress enough how important this thinking time is. Not a minute of it is wasted time. When you eventually start to write Chapter One, all the initial preparation of planning and plotting and knowing your characters will repay dividends. It's useful to get in a habit of finding slots in the day when you can think undisturbed ... while walking to the shops, in the bath, gardening. There are lots of mindless jobs, like washing-up and vacuuming, that positively fly by if you are actively engaged in thinking about your story and your characters.

No one will believe that you are actually working. A typical family comment is: 'Gazing out of the window again, I see. We don't call that work.'

But you need that thinking time. Writers who can feed in a sheet of paper and start from a blank nowhere are to be envied. The rest of us have to plot and plan. I have to think about my theme, my unique idea (is it really that unique?), the storyline, and most important of all, my characters.

You may have a brilliant plot, but if your characters are cardboard then the story will be humourless and without life. Conversely, if your characters are interesting, believable and well drawn, you could get away with a plot that is perhaps less than riveting.

People want to read about real people, to know what goes on inside their heads, their hearts, behind closed doors. They want to know them *better* than they know their spouses, their friends, their neighbours. Our immediate circle of people is an enigma. We don't really know them, what they think or why they do things. We only know what they allow us to see and often that is not very much.

But a complete and whole characterisation of a person has no secrets from us and therein lies the fascination of reading, and for us, the writing.

The beginning

This new book began when I came across a circular issued to schools on how to recognise a victim of child abuse. I did not want to write about child abuse, but, ah, I thought, there's something new and different here. There are signs, apparently: lack of concentration, withdrawal from normal activities, a watchfulness, reluctance to take part in games or swimming. I thought I could do something about these subtle signposts without going into any unpleasant or sordid details. It might alert people, teachers, mothers, friends. It might make us all more observant.

Setting

It had to be a school. Enclosed communities are always good places for stories. Hives of intrigue. Think of the number of books and plays and soaps which are set in hotels, holiday camps, housing estates, a street, a pub, wherever there is an invisible boundary and the plot cannot spill out with an evergrowing flood of ideas. This is particularly true in the writing of a thriller or murder. Keep the suspects all in one place (Agatha Christie loved house parties) and tracking the killer down is like a web tightening.

A girl's boarding school seemed obvious, an even more closed situation than a day school where the outside 'cast' might take over the story. An exclusive and expensive school would have related problems of extended families and much-married parents. I was beginning to like it very much and wanted to write it. I was starting to care ... and caring is essential.

The story was growing on me, fast. I had some experience of the school atmosphere, the excitement of sports day, the hysteria before ski-trips, the tears, the laughter, staff problems, exam nerves, runaways. I was getting almost too many ideas for one book.

The heroine/hero

All the while my heroine was taking shape too (very shapely, of course) in my mind. I saw her as a caring person, hiding her personal problems whilst working at the school. The school was her haven, her refuge from the world.

Not a teacher, perhaps the resident Sister or Matron. I saw her walking along the steep, butterfly-strewn coastal paths of South Devon, the wind in her hair, seas pounding below. She took me, not I her. This was already a case of a character becoming very much alive. I could see her high on the cliff top, windswept and breathless, an expression of loneliness on her sensitive face.

Characters do this if they are real enough in your mind. It's uncanny, surprising, rewarding. I think about them deeply. They are silent, or not so silent, companions. I keep an eye open in case I see them anywhere. Oh yes, you might easily 'see' them on a train, the underground, in a restaurant eating at the next table.

Once I saw my hero walking along Chancery Lane. I couldn't believe my eyes. Everything about this man was right, the set of his shoulders, even the same purposeful stride. I had to follow him at a discreet distance, noting every detail about him, pretending that I was going that way as well. Then it got ridiculous and I turned away, resumed my original errand. Having to leave him hurt me.

But the sight of that man was imprinted on my mind, filed away. I could always invoke this image when I was writing and it helped to make him a real person.

The next step is to find photographs. I always like photographs of my main characters pinned to the wallboard by my desk. It beats wallpaper. But photographs, you may ask? Isn't that expecting rather too much? After all, characters only exist in the mind, don't they?

No, their photographs are around, somewhere ... in glossy magazines, newspapers, the Sunday supplements. Look at the advertisements. The weekend magazines are an excellent source for those faces. Their advertisements always seem to have male models with craggy, lived-in faces doing macho things like er ... fishing or sitting on brand-new cars.

Collect, cut out and file pictures of:

- faces
- clothes
- houses
- rooms
- furniture
- meals, as served
- cars
- pets
- cities

File under simple headings, in files or brown manilla envelopes, even plastic bags. You don't have to buy a filing cabinet or start an expensive system.

But, you may say, you're writing a book, not compiling a scrap album. Agreed. What you are doing is building up the lifestyle of future characters. They are becoming flesh and blood people with homes, clothes, cars that you can describe with authority. Their lifestyle is taking shape. These visual aids are wonderful for creating an authentic atmosphere; front doors, windows, gardens, sofas, beds, carpet patterns, curtain styles, plates of gourmet cooking, names and bouquets of wines, antiques, pictures, china, glassware. It isn't possible to describe everything from memory unless you are blessed with photographic brain cells.

I'm not suggesting that you describe every item of furniture in a room, or every meal that is partaken. It would be too boring for words. Designer shopping makes yawn-yawn reading, as does meal after meal described in mouthwatering detail. Ditch the lobster bisque. It starts to look as if you collect fancy menus from hotels you haven't stayed in. Not a bad idea, but don't overdo the dill.

It does help to know what a sitting room looks like, to see the colour and texture of a favourite recipe on a plate. But we should see this through his or her eyes. We are then starting to live with our characters, not only seeing, but smelling, tasting touching, hearing.

One of my heroines lived in a big room at the top of a watertower with clover-shaped windows in each wall. It was empty except for an expensive music centre. I would never have thought of this if I had not seen an advertisement showing just such a room. I did eventually add a white sofa and a vase of daffodils for dramatic effect. (Also an ancient apple cupboard hidden in a wall.)

The same heroine needed a special long dress for a very special occasion. I found a fashion article with the perfect outfit – a straight sleek dress in dark damson velvet with a short cape lined with raspberry pink silk, matching pink gloves. My overworked imagination had been juggling with bales of material and colour swatches for days. It took a top fashion designer to design a dream outfit for my heroine.

As our setting starts to come alive and characters gather their vital statistics, it's time to prepare character charts. It's not enough to know their hair/eye colours, though it is essential to be absolutely consistent about these two visual ingredients. Write those two items of information in big letters on a card and prop on your desk:

JULIE has blue eyes/brown hair.
MAX has green eyes/black hair.

Changes of eye colour are not unknown in novels. Spotting inconsistencies is sometimes more fun than reading the book. I noticed a change of breed of pet dog in one novel; in another the same door sometimes had a bell and sometimes a knocker. Perhaps it had both, but it began to fascinate me.

Character chart

Make a chart for each important character. Fill in the information as and when it comes to you. It won't all come on the same day. Your character will grow slowly. Here are the main headings for the chart. You may think of more for yourself.

*FULL NAME	*AGE	*HEIGHT	*EYES
*HAIR	*STYLE	*SCARS	*BUILD
*SELF IMAGE	*HEALTH	*OCCUPATION	*GOALS
*POSITIVE TRAITS		*NEGATIVE TRAITS	
*AMBITION	*HOME	*FINANCE	*CAR
*HOBBIES	*FAVOURITE FOOD/COLOUR/CLOTHES		
*BAD HABITS	*FEARS	*TYPE OF HUMOUR	
*PARENTS	*FAMILY BACKGROUND		*SIBLINGS
*EDUCATION/RELIGION			

If you manage to fill in half of that chart, then you'll know a sight more about Julie than that she has blue eyes and brown hair. Add your ideas to the sample character chart and use it.

By the time I reached the stage of creating character charts for my new book, I had come across a document on the care of a bereaved child. After I read it, I knew I had all the story I wanted. Two serious themes, people with problems, a South Devon setting and a strong romance. And I'm a sucker for happy endings. Here is Troy's character chart (Fig. 6.1):

CHARACTER CHART – TROY

FULL NAME   BORN   AGE

HEIGHT   EYES   HAIR   STYLE

BUILD   SCARS   HEALTH   SELF IMAGE

OCCUPATION   GOALS

POSITIVE TRAITS

NEGATIVE TRAITS

HOME

AMBITION   HOBBIES   FINANCE   CAR

FAVOURITE FOOD/COLOUR/CLOTHES

BAD HABITS   FEARS   TYPE OF HUMOUR

PARENTS   FAMILY BACKGROUND

SIBLINGS   EDUCATIONAL/RELIGION

Why take all this trouble?

The necessity for this biographical information may not be
obvious at first. Possibly the two most important headings are
the positive and negative traits of a character. Leave lots of
space for these as they will surely grow into comprehensive
pen portraits.

A writer friend queried the need to know a character's
birthday. Surely knowing their age was sufficient, he said? But
if a book spans more than a year, then at sometime a birthday
is going to crop up, even if she dismisses it with a groan and
pulls the covers over her head. Even a birthday forgotten by
everyone is worth a mention. So decide on your characters'
birthdays. Use your own birth date.

It makes life easy if you choose dates that are already in
your family, or one that is significant to the story. Or perhaps
the date on which you start writing the book can be a timely
reminder, especially when it comes round a second time!

Yes, full name please. Why not? Most of us have full names
and we should know the full name of our character even if it
is never used. Initials are sometimes relevant.

In the same funny way, it's equally important to know the
make of the car that your hero/heroine drives. Simply getting
into a vehicle and driving off is not enough unless a complete
disinterest in things mechanical is a distinct part of their
character. Their financial situation is also of interest to the
reader. We are all curious about what people earn. How much
they are in debt, the overdraft situation, solvent or not solvent.
But it's not always sensible to state exact figures – this dates
a book faster than fashion – unless your book is a period piece
when a wage of five shillings a week is part of its charm.

Parental background, brothers and sisters, all have a bearing
on the formation of your character's personality and their
present situation. Think about your own parents and remember

their influence on your life. Your character is not born in a void, like Superman, floating down to earth in a bubble. You should know about those fictional parents even if you don't spell out every detail to your reader.

Knowing about your character's favourite foods, clothes and colours is fun though some writers may consider it trivial. Think about your own life and the part these likes and dislikes play in it. You have your favourite clothes and the disaster purchases hidden at the back of the wardrobe; your mouth may water at the thought of poached salmon and strawberries or a medium-rare steak. And colours! You wouldn't be seen dead in green. But again, your character may not care about clothes or food – so not having any interest is what needs to be known.

I enjoy giving my heroine a favourite colour and I have a stack of Matchmaker paint charts which give me wonderful shades (saffron, butterscotch, primrose, if she likes yellow). There's no need to keep using the same word.

Hairstyles are interesting, particularly if the style changes with the character's mood or even mid-novel for some reason. I scrape mine back if I'm depressed. Women are prone to using their hair as an outward sign of distress or challenge. And on a very important date, a heroine might make a special effort . . . collect illustrations from women's magazines.

Bad habits and minor flaws are what make our characters special people. Really superior people are slightly boring. Sir Lancelot du Lac became all the more believable once he fell in love with Guinevere. Eventually he became a hermit and died alone (pause for sad tears) because he was the perfect hero.

The flaw can be huge or tiny, from an uncontrollable temper, chronic untidiness (look who's talking) to something very unimportant like biting one's nails or never putting the top back on the toothpaste tube (out of date now with the new design of tube tops).

Knowing your character's health is vital. I am amazed at how many characters in books have perfect health despite the most harrowing of circumstances. Never a headache or a cold. Germs speed past breaking the sound barrier. Okay, a heroine may not look romantic with a red nose, but she's certainly more real. At least make your heroine allergic to strawberries.

Another quick word about all those course-by-course designer meals. And that's it. A quick word. They are so predictable. By all means, our characters have to eat. But what they are saying is far more interesting than what they put into their mouths.

We all have fears. Mine are violent thunderstorms overhead and people swearing at me. I die small deaths at verbal abuse. Fortunately neither happens often. We might be afraid of heights, spiders, failure, getting stuck in lifts, being embarrassed in front of friends, saying the wrong thing. Don't we all do it? I'm always saying the wrong thing. (Is there a cupboard in which I can hide?) Some of us are afraid of being made to look a fool or having to speak publicly. It's not simply a major fear of death, accident or illness. ('I'm not afraid of dying; I just don't want to be around when it happens' - Woody Allen.) It's the small fears of life which make our characters real.

Are you beginning to see why a character chart can be such a help? Keep it handy, refer to it when you need to check. It'll save time in the long run if you are absolutely 100 per cent sure that your hero does not take sugar every time he begins to stir a coffee.

7

TITLES AND OTHER FIRSTS

The first of all the firsts is the title. Next in importance comes the opening paragraph, then the first page and the first chapter. Work and rework these pages until they glow. They set the tone for your whole book; they sell it.

The title

The title is like a headline that declares the image of your story. So write a stylish title. It should contain the essence of your book, say what it is about. Invent a title that makes it stand out from the hundreds of other titles, shoulder to shoulder on the bookshelf at W. H. Smith's. I repeat this deliberately because it is so important. Such a lot depends on your title. But unless it comes to you in a blinding flash and you know that it's instantly right, then the title is something to sweat tears over.

The title is the first of the firsts that has got to grab the editor or publisher. She'll be keener to carry on reading your book if it has a good title, a fascinating opening, a page-turning first chapter.

This book weathered at least five titles: i.e. it changed with the weather. *How to Plan, Plot and Polish*; *How to Plot and*

Use a Synopsis; *How to Write a Successful Synopsis*; *Plotting a Synopsis that Sells*; *Plotting Plus* . . . and I'm still thinking.

A title should have rhythm and be easy to say and remember as well as telling the reader what the book is about and what they can expect to read. If you buy a glitzy airport paperback called *Brocade*, you would know instantly that it isn't a handbook on dressmaking. Clothes may feature in it, but not the nitty-gritty of cutting, tacking, and how to put in a zip.

Apparently people love the sound of the consonants M, K, G and P in a title. Don't ask me why. And I shouldn't let it bother you. *The Eagle has Landed* managed without them, and so did *The Day of the Jackal*.

But let's think how important titles are with their imagery and suggestion of plot. Do you think these titles would have become bestsellers? *Scarlett's Adventures Down South*? *Father Ralph and his Obsessive Ambition*? *Jolly Polo Sticks*? *Gabriel Oak and Bathsheba*? *A Mini Encyclopedia of Household Management*? *Lilliput's Unusual Prisoner*? They are not instant, eye-catching titles, although we know that the content of each book is eminently readable. Now some more might-have-been titles . . . hold on, this is getting too much fun. I'm supposed to be working. Think of others for yourself.

Rhythm

There is a fashion for one-word titles at the moment, but it will probably pass. Two-word titles have the most rhythm and seem to stay in the mind. Words with two or three syllables have a kind of flow . . . *Virgin Soldiers*, *Whisky Galore*, *Eastern Approaches*, *Peter Abelard*. And each of those titles makes an announcement.

The title should come from within your book; the story itself often suggests one to you, or you suddenly see it already written in the text. It just needs spotting. *Gone with the Wind* is taken from the text and was only found after a long search by Margaret Mitchell and her publisher for a good title.

If you become really stuck over a title and it's holding you up, then there are three steps to take:

- Give it a one-word working title
- Hand the problem over to your unconscious
- Try lists

Sometimes I feel I can't even start a book or a short story because it doesn't have the right title. This can hold me up for weeks while I search through the Bible, my dictionary of quotations and proverbs, the racing pages. Horses have amazing racing names ... Titch Wizard, Tactical Mission, Timeless Times, Gone Savage, Crystal Jack ... and that's only from today's newspaper.

Quotations are another brilliant source for titles, and so is the quiz game *Catchphrase* on television. Page-turning through a dictionary of quotations and proverbs always suggests dozens of titles, perhaps not the right one for a particular book, but ones that you long to use another time.

Open it at random. Page 316. Immediately I find: *Burning Daylight*; *Angels Wooing*; *Farewell Goes out Sighing*; *The Speaking Foot*; *Mine Oyster*; *Chance or Death* ... all from *The Merry Wives of Windsor* and *Troilus and Cressida* (Shakespeare). None appropriate for this book (wait, *Burning Daylight* might be – a subtle alternative to *Midnight Oil*? ... I like it).

Making lists is another way of finding a title. I found the title *The Secret Taj* by this method. I made three separate lists of single words. The first list was of strong nouns that had a prominence in the story; the second list was of adjectives that also had some relevance; the third list contained the mysterious element of the theme. Then I cross linked them from one list to another, any way, any order, stirring the words. Titles came from all directions. Then suddenly the right one appeared out of the muddle ... *The Secret Taj*.

But if all fails at the beginning, give your book a working title – anything that will identify it from your other work – and start planning, plotting and writing. It won't feel completely right but it's better than waiting around for inspiration. Take heart, for your unconscious is working on it.

Our unconscious works mostly while we are asleep. It's really nice to think that our other self is beavering away while we are unwrinkling our faces. Twice I have presented my unconscious with a title problem, and twice the perfect title has popped into my mind some days later when I wasn't thinking about it at all.

For my crime story I wanted a title from the marriage service but all the best phrases had already been used ... *Dearly Beloved*, *To Have and To Hold*, *Till Death Us Do Part*. There is no copyright in titles but I wanted to be original. So that I could get on with writing the book, I called it *Let No Man*, a pretty dreadful title. It has no rhythm; it's stilted and meaningless. I didn't like it.

I had written the book, revised and revised, polished every word and printed it out. Two years of work and the manuscript was ready to go to my agent, but it wasn't going anywhere with that title. It had to have something a hundred times better before I would deliver it.

That night, before going to sleep, I explained the dilemma to my unconscious and hoped it would come up with some suggestions. Three days later as I was walking through Victoria Station, a title popped into mind. It was *the* title, complete, perfect ... *Lucifer's Bride*. A bride fit for a fallen archangel, the devil himself. It was just right. I almost could see the cover ...

The hook

The opening paragraph must contain a hook of some kind to grab the reader's interest, a special something that holds her attention in its crab-like claws. She must want to read on. This paragraph should signal, however obliquely, some information that gives the reader a clue as to the content of the book.

Take a cold look at your first paragraph. Often it is not needed at all. Maybe your story actually begins further on so don't waste time by starting slowly in first gear. Slam in the clutch and roar off in top.

The first page is also important. It's what makes a reader buy the book or borrow it from the library. Watch people at the bookshops when they pick up a book. This is what they do:

- Read the title, glance at the cover and author's name. (Who?)
- Turn it over and read the blurb on the back cover.
- Flick through the book to see if they like the distribution of black and white (i.e. whether it's all narrative or all dialogue or an acceptable mixture of both).
- Then, if interested, open the first page and read the first few paragraphs.

If the first paragraph is boring, the transaction will probably go no further. Back goes the book on the shelf. A sale is often as simple as that.

It is usually on those four pieces of information that a reader decides whether to buy a book or not. Since few authors have any control over the cover or the blurb, then it's up to us to make the title and the opening paragraph the very best possible.

The opening paragraph has several functions. It should, if possible, show the main character in action, hint at what is to come, set the tone of the story, promise the reader that the strands of the plot are going to collide. A tall order for one paragraph. If you can manage two of those premises, then you are doing well.

My own favourite opening paragraph is from Mary Stewart's *Touch Not the Cat*:

My lover came to me on the last night in April, with a message and a warning that sent me home to him.

Note the contradiction ... her lover came to her in the night and yet he can't be there because she says she has to go home to him! Wonderful stuff ... plus a message and a warning. Obviously style No. 7 in the following list.

There are nine styles of opening paragraph which are frequently used:

- Weather forecasts
- Moment of change
- Shock, horror
- Dialogue
- Scenic
- Lo and Behold
- Mysterious
- Action
- Introspective

A few quick examples, not from published novels, but just to illustrate the list:

1. 'It was raining hard. Rain flooded the pavements and sent the shoppers hurrying for shelter; the gutters were overflowing with a flotilla of sodden debris.'

There is nothing wrong with that opening as a picture of a wet shopping street. But where's the hook? How about adding four words 'and sent ALL BUT ONE OF the shoppers hurrying for shelter'. Immediately you think, why, who?

2. 'She took the new baby into her arms. Life would never be the same. Now she had to work and think for two, and she would do that, even though the baby was not hers.'

Plenty there.

3. 'The guillotine fell with a sickening thud . . .' etcetera.

4. ' "I'm not staying," he said, flinging open the door. "And I don't care if you're dying. Don't expect me at the funeral." '

5. 'The Yorkshire moors rolled into misty distance, timeless and intriguing, their secrets hidden in dells and valleys and guarded by the small streams that burbled innocently between the rocks.'

Add one word . . . BARELY hidden . . . and there's a new dimension.

6. 'Time waited in the wings as it had for centuries, relentlessly watching the players . . .'

Pass me an aspirin.

7. Sorry, I can't improve on Mary Stewart's opening paragraph. Read it again and see how clever it is.

8. 'He climbed the wall steathily, the knife hidden in the sleeve of his leather jacket. He had exactly two and a half minutes in which to find his target and get out.'

Ticking clock.

9. 'The lone woman stood at the end of the harbour, watching the ferry leave for France. She wondered if she would have the strength to walk away; no one knew how much it had cost her to be there in the first place.'

The first page

The first page should contain three promises: that there is going to be an intriguing or memorable situation, indicate who are the main characters, and set the tone for the novel so that the reader knows whether she is in for a romance, a thriller, a sexy shopping saga, science fiction or adventure. The first page is a contract with the reader. I, the author, promise you, the reader, this kind of story.

It should be written and rewritten until it is right. This is time well spent.

Romance

This genre demands that the heroine is introduced straight away. Even on the first page there is going to be something about her that intrigues us and we are going to get a strong hint of the basic conflict ahead.

Here are the first two paragraphs of my book *Daughter of Tor*:

> She tugged at the sash of the old-fashioned window and threw it open, letting the sea wind cool her overheated brow. Troy was angry. Grace was making her give up her home and it was not fair.
>
> 'I'm having to move out, lock, stock and bottles of good French wine, at two days' notice. Can you believe it, tree? And all because of a man.'

Look how much we can learn from those few lines. The heroine's name is Troy. That's unusual. She lives by the sea. She is very fond of her home. She is lively and spirited, has a good sense of humour. The conflict is already planted because Grace is making her move out - for the sake of some man, a total stranger. It is obvious that the man is

70

going to play an important part in Troy's life and the story.

And she's talking to a tree? This lady is certainly different. Shades of Prince Charles. All this in two paragraphs.

Mainstream/crime/murder

For these we want more of the setting. We need to see, touch, smell, be in the place where the story starts. We want to feel the atmosphere, whether it's a sleepy (drowsy is a better word) village, a dynamic and powerful business, a bustling city, a steamy foreign location. Each of these clichés conjures up a stereotype place but it's then that the writer, and the writer's style and inner thoughts imprint the setting with an uniqueness. The reader needs to be able to identify with the place, to say: 'yes, that could happen there – or here'.

The main character does not have to appear on the first page; it could be the victim or a subsidiary character if he really contributes to the story. The reader needs to know fairly soon if it's the kind of murder story with a sleuth, amateur or professional. But here, the canvas is much broader and really anything goes, as long as it hooks, gives some information, begins the story with some intriguing situation or thought. Don't be bland or boring. These are the opening paragraphs of *Lucifer's Bride*:

When Adele Kimberley meticulously planned her elder daughter's wedding, she was hoping it would be the wedding of the year. And that's exactly what it became. The wedding of the year.

She did not know that the tin cans would never clatter down the drive, the carnival streamers never stream and the decorated vintage car, despite its effortless battalion horsepower speed, would not go anywhere at all.

From this we learn three important things: that the wedding goes seriously wrong; that Adele and family are well off and she is ambitious - wedding of the year, a drive to the house, a vintage car; there's a hint of imminent disaster, of coming notoriety. There's also another daughter. Quite a lot of information in two paragraphs.

The fashion for a slow, leisurely beginning with a long description of a place, the weather, or some family background has gone. There is not the time nor the market for leisurely, slow starts. Readers want to be into the story right away. Like instant food, they want instant story.

Chapter One

The first chapter is the pivot of the whole story. It's no use Chapter Five being wonderful; no one will reach it if Chapter One is not exciting, intriguing, and arouses our interest or curiosity. Who is going to wade through four chapters to get to the best bit, fifty pages on? Not the publisher's reader.

This chapter is going to be full of information for the reader, and I don't mean pages of narrative and all your research notes. It should:

- Set the tone of the book and tell the reader whether it's going to be a romance, crime, science fiction, etc.
- Introduce your main characters by name, showing them as vital and interesting. Describe their looks briefly, but also show their personality, good and weak traits, making them real people.

- Establish the setting, the atmosphere, letting the reader identify with this fictional world.
- Indicate the coming conflict, the main problem, intrigue, mystery, crime, romance, action. Plant clues as to what is going to happen.
- If it's a romance, then there must be an immediate meeting between the hero and heroine and the first signs of conflict must be apparent. At the same time, there should be an undercurrent of sexual chemistry between them. A moment of recognition. In cricketing terms, it's MCC ... meeting, chemistry and conflict.
- Include good, strong dialogue between the main characters with the dialogue revealing their emotional state. Let us into their thoughts.
- Back story should be confined to a few flashback scenes. More can be added, in small doses, as the story progresses.
- Any secondary characters should be introduced briefly.
- End the chapter on a real high. Make it a page turner.

Openings to avoid

- Don't start with a long description of the background to the story with nothing happening. It works better if the landscape or environment is seen through a character's eyes.
- Arriving at an airport, coming in to land, flying off somewhere in a big jumbo jet. The flying scene has been overdone and it has become the pet hate of many publishers.
- Try to avoid opening with a really sad and depressing scene ... someone dying of cancer, a suicide, drug addiction, funeral of a parent or child.

- Character asleep, dreaming, or half-awake, recalling long stretches of childhood.
- Anything weird or incomprehensible. If an opening is too much of a puzzle, the reader will tire of the book and give up before it has a chance to enchant.

By now you will realise how important all these firsts are in the writing of your book. In the excitement of plotting a new story, a story that you really care about, the first chapter should not be thought of as a hurdle but as the beginning of a personal adventure into the unknown.

8

THE OGRE OF WRITER'S BLOCK

Some writers never get writer's block. They don't know how lucky they are. For others, it is an ever-present monster, prowling round the fringes of their mind, setting traps that they fall into every time.

A colleague of mine says the answer is a double whisky. I prefer white wine fast chilled with an ice cube. But it isn't that simple, though there is a long line of writers who find alcohol loosens the creative juices. Alcohol for them is the oil that makes the motor run smoothly. They don't have writer's block, just creaking joints.

There are three categories of writer's block and degrees of self-help which can banish them, if not forever, long enough for your confidence to return:

- simple daily reluctance to start writing
- problems in storyline
- total loss of creative ability

The first is only temporary, self-inflicted, and can be treated with a certain degree of light-heartedness and tolerance. We all hate starting work, the actual discipline of making ourselves sit down and begin the process of writing. Some writers have obsessions, rituals, before they can get going - like sharpening all their pencils, tidying their desk. I can't even find my desk

- is it somewhere under all that paper? My tidying is accomplished like Christmas, once a year and in a devil of a rush, most usefully executed with a flourish just before I start a new piece of work and need the luxury of some decent space.

So let's look at ways of getting started in the morning/ evening, whichever is your regular working time. It helps to begin work at the same time each day, every day. A pattern is useful. We are creatures of habit, if you'll pardon the cliché . . . sometimes it's necessary to use them. My time is 10 a.m., which gives me a chance to do an hour's mad housework, but I drop the duster on the stroke of ten.

Under starter's orders

- Make a cup of coffee
- Switch on word processor or uncover typewriter
- Put in disc or sheet of typing paper
- Read what you wrote yesterday

Reading what you last wrote is the crucial key. Read yourself into your current piece of work by going over yesterday's writing. You will find yourself unconsciously editing, improving, adding a word or two and by the time your coffee has cooled, you'll be back in harness.

Of course, it isn't always as easy as this. Sometimes even then you are stumped and unable to get going. So do some warm-ups . . .

- Write nonsense
- Write about the weather
- Write some dialogue with your main characters in a totally new situation.

And I do mean write nonsense. Here goes ... Oh look folks, I'm totally stuck, I'm up the creek, I haven't a clue what to write next. I'd really rather be out in the garden. Doesn't the garden look nice? The Japanese maple is uncurling its leaves like raspberry feathers and the lethal laburnum is hanging its golden poison in heavy clusters. Why don't those lethal seeds poison the ground? Why do primroses still grow under it? *Killing All the Primroses*. Perhaps that's a title. I wonder if I could use it?

I promise you that is genuine nonsense. I wrote anything that came into my head, but already thoughts and ideas are flowing and if I were not writing about writer's block, I'd be thinking about the demise of primroses. Acres of them. Fields of primroses. Giant primroses? Perhaps a certain kind of flower that thrives on poison ...

This nonsense – which is just a run-in for the day, like revving the engine before you let off the handbrake – can be deleted later, thrown away. It has served a purpose.

Writing about the weather is the same kind of exercise, but it need not be deleted if it usefully contributes to the story. The British are obsessed by the weather. We all want to know what's happening to our erratic climate. Snow in April. Heatwaves in November. Try to write something different, let your imagination take off. Some words automatically drag the same adjectives to themselves ... balmy breezes, misty mornings ...

Inventing a totally new situation and making your characters talk about it can bring a stale story to life. Choose something simple: they are at a bus stop waiting for a bus. Write the dialogue. Your characters will take over, talk, argue, snap at each other ... perhaps they'll suddenly say something you'd never expected and that's exciting. Extra dialogue:

'I'm going to be late.'

'Your own fault for taking so long to get ready. I've

never known anyone who needs half an hour in the shower. What are you doing, learning to swim vertically?'

'Oh, you're so funny. It's a wonder you're not on *Wogan*. In the audience. The moron with the loud laugh.'

'I can't believe that once I thought you were sweet, delightful woman. How you've changed.'

'You don't have to look far to find what changed me. That shop window will do.'

'Typical snide – I don't believe it. Across the road, don't look. Look at the reflection in the shop window. Isn't that . . . with . . .?'

'It is. I wish I hadn't seen them . . .'

Leave that intriguing situation and go back to your storyline with your characters very much alive and talking to each other and doing things.

Much later, delete the fake bus-stop situation. It was only a device to wake up your characters.

Dead ends and blind alleys

This is a little more serious, not just the morning hiccup. You may have had too many interruptions or become a slave to distractions. You may be depressed by rejections and the fear of failing. Your favourite editor may have left – they do seem to change jobs rather frequently. Your story has ground to a halt and you are left worried and wondering.

Firstly, don't panic. It happens to everyone at some time. We all have doubts about our ability to ever write again or the worth of what we are writing. Take some deliberate time off, just a few days. Walk, read, swim . . . be active as well as leisurely. Writing is a sedentary occupation (unless, like

Hemingway, you write standing up) and some physical activity will give you a glow. Be kind to yourself, pretend you are convalescing from an obscure but unthreatening illness.

Sometimes we write ourselves to a standstill and deserve a break. A short holiday could be the answer. A brisk walk along a cliff top or a wave-lashed shingle beach can blow away any amount of stuffy writer's blues. A weekend in Cumbria, walking and climbing, letting the endless views heal a tired mind . . . a writer's course somewhere when you talk shop with like-minded people and collect sympathy.

I notice all sorts of things when I'm walking . . . an ant carrying something almost as large as itself . . . the roots of a tree, centuries old, distorted by the October storm . . . the sudden breath-taking beauty of a kestrel hovering in the sky. Nature never fails to sharpen my awareness of the world.

Walk the dog, walk the cat, walk the budgie. Walking and reading are the ailing writer's remedies.

When you return to your desk, refreshed and hungry to start work again, re-read your previous chapters. If it is still not working, then you need to go back to the drawing board and find out where you are going wrong. Ask yourself these questions:

- Do you really know your characters?
- Have you enough plot to sustain your story?
- Is the motivation of your characters truly thought through?
- Are you writing the right book for you?
- Do you really care about this book and care about the characters?

If the honest answer to this last question is No, then you are writing the wrong book and no amount of re-working is going to help. Put it away and start something new. Look through your notebook of ideas and see what really excites you.

If the answer is Yes, then perhaps you have cut corners on your homework and you don't really know enough about your characters and their motivation for doing things. Maybe your storyline is thin. It needs a little extra something.

So write a character sketch of your main characters. If you come to a halt after a simple physical description (blue eyes, brown hair), then you don't know them. Have a look at Chapter Six and fill at least a page about each character.

Play the What-if? game with your plot. Come up with at least ten alternative what-if ideas, the wilder the better. They are all a stimulation of the imagination, and stepping stones in a new direction.

If you don't know the What-if? game, then let's play it. It's a form of lateral thinking, thoughts going along different routes. The situation could be the morning after a disastrous date. Setting: heroine in her kitchen. Begin with simple, low-key what if ideas, such as:

- She makes a cup of coffee
- She falls over the cat
- She drops the coffee and scalds herself
- He phones and she refuses to answer the phone
- There's an accident outside and she rushes out thinking it's him
- Her mother arrives, saying she's seen him throwing suitcases in his car and driving off at speed
- She sees a newsflash on television that two ferries have collided
- She hurries to find him but her car won't start
- A gas main explodes in the street
- Your turn ... think up the tenth what-if situation yourself

Inventing a whole group of alternatives gives you two sets of decisions to make: those which you throw out instantly as being unsuitable and those which have possibilities if reworked in a different way. Small changes could make all the difference. Check back to your synopsis and outline to make sure the changes don't wreck the overall plot. The story is moving of its own accord and even you don't know what's happening. Perhaps you are ready to start writing again.

You could decide to use two of your 'what-if' ideas – maybe the cup of coffee and the newsflash – inserting the information that he was going to travel by ferry that day earlier into the story. Now we have an interesting situation, not merely a disastrous date.

Total depression

There is no way of being light-hearted about a total, mind-blowing writer's block. For a writer, this is a devastating nightmare. The light of life has gone out. What is there left to do in the darkness?

I have never experienced this and, please God, I hope I never will. Writing is my obsession, the joy of my life, my passion, and without it, I really don't know how I would live. I suppose I would give a home to several more cats, eat far too many hand-made Belgian chocolates, watch too much mindless television and feel the loss acutely.

Emotional trauma of some kind is usually the cause of complete writer's block . . . bereavement, divorce, an accident, ill health. All these things need time to get over and this is what you must give yourself. Time, my friend. Do not despair. Life is always changing and it will change again for you. Sometimes a field must lie fallow.

But many writers find that writing is a therapy in difficult situations.

A friend of mine came home from her husband's funeral and wrote a short story that afternoon. It did not mean she was not upset or was a callous woman; she knew that writing would help her. Writing was her solace.

The daughter of another friend was in a terrible accident. Fiction-writing was impossible. This writer had just been commissioned to write a true-fact book and keeping that 31 December deadline was her lifeline. Being professional she had to keep it. She wrote so much each month and no more. The rest of her time was devoted to her daughter. The book was delivered on the dot.

But what if you can't reorganise your life to take in this new situation and your mind has closed itself to writing? Like enduring pain, I would say ... relax, go with it. Accept the block, don't be bitter, don't fight it. This is your fallow time.

What do fallow fields do? Absolutely nothing. Don't feel guilty. Do absolutely nothing. Don't take on more guilt if a blank and dusty screen sits idle on your desk. Put some flowers on your desk instead.

Fallow fields gather up nutrients. So read. Read everything in sight. What bliss to have the time to read and read, the luxury of it. Feel luxurious and browse in libraries and bookshops, come home with armfuls.

Do the things you've always wanted to do but never had the time ... go to meetings and stately homes, go on a coach tour and look at gardens, go to the theatre, the cinema, horse racing. Seek out little museums in small market towns; look at places in England you've never seen. This country has hundreds of villages, teeming with history, all worth visiting and exploring. Take the tourist track and see for free what the foreign visitors pay huge air fares to come over and visit.

Keep in touch with your writing friends and go to some weekend conferences, even if you are not writing. At least they will understand how you are feeling when no one else does.

One day there will be a stirring inside you, something so vague you'll hardly notice it, like the very first crack in the ice. The thought will come that you want to write again, but now, after so long, you are terrified.

Terrified of failure. It's nothing new. We all feel that fear at times. But you, dear blocked-up writer, are special and need a linguistic inhaler.

Take the Dorothy Brande treatment once a day, prefereably first thing in the morning, with a cup of hot tea. She says, in her wonderful book for writers, *Becoming a Writer*, that writing something, anything, in a notebook after waking from sleep, is the best way to start the day.

Keep this notebook by the side of your bed and write something every morning. No one is going to see what you write, random thoughts, dreams, descriptions, vent your anger, despair, your grief. It's a five-finger exercise. If you hadn't played the piano for a year, you couldn't immediately give a Mozart concert in the Albert Hall.

Then, another day, when you feel like it . . . no hurry . . . get out a musty dog-eared manuscript that was abandoned years ago. You are not going to make yourself write. No, instead you are going to retype it or put it on disc. Just a few pages. Poor neglected, forgotten old story. Your editing mind will take over, just a little at first, a word here, a word there, a scrap of dialogue brought up to date. You might even enjoy what you are doing . . . after all, it's only typing.

Is the ice still cracking?

Write very small things at first. A poem. Perhaps only eight lines. Have you ever written a poem? They are so satisfying. No one is going to see it, those lines straight from the heart, funny, nostalgic, poignant. They are personal. Put them away with your dreams.

Play around with ideas for a very short story. Have a try. Eight hundred words can't bite you. What does it matter if you throw it away? But I bet you don't. And what was that idea you had for a novel, that newspaper cutting, those holiday brochures you filed away, that marvellous twist ending you never used?

By now the fallow field will be bursting with the promise of new growth and the paralysis will have gone. And with it the ogre of writer's block. Banished to the dark forest.

9

THE JOY OF POLISHING

Polishing means honing to a diamond-sharp perfection. Cut, weigh, hone and polish your words. Treat every phrase as a precious stone which has to be polished to a brilliant sparkle. Some people call it revision, but polishing sounds less depressing and we should never feel negative about our work.

Honing brings with it a deal of anguish, and there's a lot of that going on when it's necessary to cut, cut and cut again. As we re-read our work, we yearn to have written better, pine for lost inspiration, moan as we spot lapses and mistakes, grieve as we have to ruthlessly hack at a well-written piece that does not really fit or add anything to the story.

Each word, phrase, sentence, paragraph, has to be judged and weighed for its contribution to the prose. If found wanting, then it should be replaced by something better or cut completely. Judicious pruning never hurt a rose bush.

When to begin

The long arduous task of the first draft is over; polishing, once a distant, housework-type word, is now your first concern. For months you have been stimulated to write this fascinating story and you have let it run ... and run. It is with immense pride and pleasure that you type THE END and reach wearily for a large gin and tonic or the remote control or both.

Do it. Take time off. It's necessary to let your MS cool and settle into its own shape. You wouldn't cut a cake straight from the oven while it was hot. You have finished your draft and deserve a breathing space before beginning that solid second-draft rewriting.

Some authors never touch a word once it is written. There was certainly a good fairy at their christenings and her name was Confidence. They send off their MS straight from the word processor, no tampering, no tinkering, word perfect from day one. It is a gift. The rest of us have to work and work to achieve what we hope is our very best.

Leave your short story for a few days or a week, longer for a novel. You need to create an intellectual distance. Start something else, walk the dog, feed the family, invent a new filing system. It's ideal to have a holiday ahead or planned break as your self-imposed deadline for finishing, then you can cheerfully go off on your hols, knowing that you finished your MS on time and there's no need to be ridden with guilt now that you are not working.

Of course, while on your hols/weekend break, you are making notes. All writers are compulsive note-takers. Never move more than a few yards from your house without a small notebook and a pen. I once posted a letter to a friend with scribbles on the back. She phoned me up. 'What's all this gibberish on the envelope?' she wanted to know. I had thought of a line of dialogue on the way to the postbox with no paper handy.

In this cooling-off period, it's useful to jot down anything that comes to mind that you want to remember for your book, all those afterthoughts. You know the kind of thing . . .

- check weather at the wedding
- have I been consistent about time of service?

- find out how fuse works
- what happens to the dog?

Check those things now. It'll save time later to have another big sheet of paper with all the notes together.

But don't start tinkering. Don't ever tinker. Anxious tinkering can ruin what was a perfectly good first draft. Fiction fatigue often sets in after a long sustained effort and the mind is in no fit state to make good decisions.

The craft of polishing

Polishing becomes a sort of sixth sense. You do it all the time, as you go along; and you do it again when the first draft is finished. You know what you are doing without having to use a checklist. The more you polish, the more it becomes second nature.

If there were a polishing checklist for the ongoing checks and for checking the first draft, it would first of all remind us to:

- cut for length
- cut unnecessary adjectives, adverbs
- cut superfluous words
- tighten phrases
- check lengths of paragraphs
- check smoothness of paragraph transitions
- use more evocative words.

My own pattern of working is to revise the previous day's work on disc very briefly each morning, before starting on new writing. This is a kind of 'reading and writing in' process which is valuable. But it is by no means my only stage of polishing.

My main polishing – in longhand – starts when the first draft is printed out and I can see it on a page.

I enjoy the process of polishing. The hard graft of putting down whole masses of words from scratch is over. In the summer the garden beckons and I can sit with a chapter or two on my knee and work it over and over again, thinking it word by word, sentence by sentence, the balance of dialogue and narrative. It's the business of decisions, so that every phrase is the best that is possible.

Polishing the draft

Polishing the first draft has its own creative excitement, although it is essentially about choice and selection. One can usually see the padding early on. A bit of writing that carried you along in the wrong direction or a character that has no business being there. Perhaps you were tired. Perhaps it was very late. It's pretty painless to delete there and then, before it becomes major surgery.

The basic things that you have to do in the main polishing exercise are:

- cut out the padding – edit
- invent – fill in the gaps
- strengthen – put more flesh on skinny bones
- check – facts, dialogue, repetition . . . and continuity.

Cutting

The object of cutting is to tighten the prose, to be ruthlessly self-critical. Look upon it as a slimming process, leaving the muscle, the flesh and the bones, but eliminating all the flab.

Cut absolutely everything that has nothing to do with your story. But cut wisely. Don't hack, mangle, tear out the roots or you won't have anything left.

Weak or sketchy work should go. All those useless, extra words must go ... only, just, always, had, really, even, almost, all, usually ... and so on. *Just* is my ogre. I write it in everywhere. She *just* made a cup of tea. She *just* closed the door. She *just* hated him. It creeps in without my even noticing. Help! There's another one. See what I mean? That 'even' adds nothing.

Sometimes whole scenes have to go or an entire character must be removed from a scene ... a superfluous secretary, an intrusive waiter. This is hard and it's a pity that they were not spotted earlier as being unnecessary.

Cutting for required length is hard work, but should have been part of your initial planning. Always keep a running check on the word length of each chapter. It can save a lot of the heartbreak which comes if later you realise you have overrun by 10,000 words.

Inventing

Maybe your book needs new scenes, new dialogue, new twists to the tale. Time now to put them in with – very sparingly some exposition. Exposition is like explanation, the writing that is the least like action. Extra necessary research can be inserted, but not much. Research should be like an iceberg – only a limited amount showing.

Perhaps in your mad rush to get the first draft down, you left out a whole chunk of story which, it's now painfully obvious, must be there or the plot won't make sense. You'll have to do it. Start writing again, but now it is far less of a chore because that awkward scene has the scaffolding of the rest of the story to hold it up.

Strengthening

Strengthening means putting flesh on the bones of your plot, filling out your characters into real people. You knew it had to be done sometime but were in too much of a hurry to do it earlier because you wanted to get on. The story has started talking back to you, telling you what it needs, and you're making a mental note, or better still, writing notes on a sheet of cardboard propped on your desk.

From this new emotional distance you see lots of things that can be brought out, buried information that your unconscious had put in the story for you to discover. It's such fun when this happens.

In the first draft of my crime story, *Lucifer's Bride*, I discovered red herrings I didn't realise I had planted (sorry about the mixed metaphor); an added motive which was perfect; an explosive new twist. I couldn't believe my luck. They improved the story and they had been there all the time waiting for me to notice.

Make strong scenes stronger with extra lines of dialogue, more powerful verbs, vigorous action, dynamic thoughts. This is your chance to strengthen an undeveloped scene that seems to wobble on the page. Don't say 'she went out', say 'she rushed out', or, better still, 'she fled'.

By the end of the first draft you'll know your characters pretty well, so find ways of fleshing out characters so that the reader will know them as intimately as you. Thoughts will come to you naturally as you go through each page. Yes, of course, she would have thought this here; his reaction would be that there; they would have followed this course of action, not that.

This distancing makes it possible to see patterns emerging. Echoes, circles, mirrors of things that happened earlier, happening again, making satisfactory ripples. *You're cleverer than you thought you were.* You were actually too close to see it happening at first. Now these patterns can be focused and the echoes made more vibrant, the mirrors more accurate, the circles complete.

Your best writing is often done at this later stage. There is time for that considered thought, searching for exactly the right phrase, the right word, an original simile. You are not in quite such a rush. The garden is peaceful, the dragonflies darting, butterflies like drifts of coloured snow and the right thoughts are hovering in your mind in much the same way.

Knowing what has to be done is a slow learning process. We learn by trial and error, to use a cliché. But since it is a draft we are working on, it doesn't matter how many times we cross something out and try a new phrase, a new word, something more intriguing.

Checking

This is your chance to check facts and to make sure that everything in your story is consistent. Check the spelling of characters' names, place names, house names. When a work is over-familiar to you, it's surprising how easy it is for it to change – 'Anne' to become 'Ann' without you noticing, or 'Shrublands' to become 'Oaklands' without moving a brick.

Check ages, physical descriptions, and in particular, any defect. If he's left-handed or wears glasses, make sure there's

91

no miraculous metamorphosis halfway through the story. Check dates of known events, bus routes, train journeys. A story was once ruined for me because I knew the heroine was starting her journey from the wrong London terminus. We often make mental reminders whilst writing at speed. 'I'll check that later,' we say ... then promptly forget. Mark it on the draft in big letters. CHECK. Or make a checklist as you write in draft or every item that needs checking and work your way through it in odd moments.

(Remember to put page numbers on every item. Page 89 – icebergs – Ency. This means that on Page 89, I must check about icebergs in an encyclopaedia.)

Dialogue

While economy is the key to good dialogue, avoid writing it in a kind of verbal shorthand. The reverse is also true. In real life, we ramble, waffle on about nothing, speak in half-finished sentences. All this has to be tidied up or cut out.

The principal functions of dialogue are:

- to convey the character of our story actors
- to convey any necessary information that advances the plot
- to show the emotional state of the speaker

Check whether each line of dialogue achieves at least one of these functions. If not, perhaps it should be cut. Pointless chats about the weather and shopping are like trying to read porridge.

And dialogue should have a rhythm. If a line of dialogue doesn't seem right, try saying it out loud. You may feel foolish at first, but it does help. My characters speak in my head, especially when I'm swimming. They act out scenes in front of me as I swim up and down 25-metre lengths.

Real dialogue is peppered with repetitions, long pauses and tautology. Tautology is the use of words to repeat a meaning already conveyed. If this realism creeps into your fictional dialogue, cut it out. Write what seems natural, but keep it crisp and short. Don't waste words. There isn't room for irrelevancies. And watch out for overlong sentences. We don't talk in paragraphs.

Repetition

It is only too easy to repeat words and phrases, even similar situations keep popping up. The same adjectives and adverbs can pepper out prose without our noticing first time around. But during revision these adjectives and adverbs should leap off the page, ringing alarm bells. Cut or find a better word. *Roget's Thesaurus* is the writer's friend. Learn how to use this wonderful book. Put it on your Christmas list.

Repeating the name of a character too often is another weakness that can be tidied up. Use 'he' or 'she' if it's perfectly clear who is present and the situation is not confusing with a lot of characters milling around. In an exchange of dialogue between two characters, their names can be edited out completely as long as it is perfectly clear who is talking. It might be necessary to insert a short sentence of thought or action, just to remind the reader who is speaking.

Clarity and accuracy

This is the opportunity to get rid of clumsy phrases, those

useless words that creep in – always, just, etc. – the forests of dead-wood padding. Time to correct any inaccurate facts, inconsistencies, lapses of memory. Writers have been known to introduce pets which never get fed or taken for walks, change makes of cars mid-story, send a heroine to the library on a Sunday, state the obvious . . . 'he crawled on all fours'.

I love them. We are all human. We make mistakes.

Maximise curiosity

Many writers in the throes of crafting a novel forget the value of producing a page-turner. It's worth looking once more at the opening and ending of every chapter. Every chapter should end with some lines of drama, revelation, intrigue that make the reader want to continue reading instead of putting out the light.

When she does turn the page, the beginning of the next chapter should not disappoint her with a dull or formal beginning. Every chapter must have a bold beginning . . . weather forecasts and cups of tea are out. You've planted a bait at the end of the previous chapter, now hook your reader with the beginning of the next. Dialogue often makes a good start, or go straight into the action, introspective or physical.

It pays to look at each chapter in cold isolation to see if the first page and last page work as page-turners. Be the reader reading it for the first time. Would you want to read on? If not, why not? Analyse what has gone wrong and try some alternatives. Sometimes a very small alteration in a sentence can suddenly give it a different meaning.

You cannot spend too much time revising and polishing. There, now, I've said it. Revising and polishing. They go together like fish and chips. You can't have one without the other. The inexact word must be replaced by the exact word;

every adjective and adverb must be scrutinised for its worth. Clumsy sentences must be made to flow.

Give your manuscript an elegance and eloquence. Give it a shape and remember that spaces can speak.

Editorial revision

This is a different kind of revision. You've done your own polishing and submitted the manuscript. If an editor at the publishing house likes your manuscript, she may suggest some changes. Perhaps she thinks there should be more dialogue or more about the growing relationship between the hero and the heroine. She may think that the background distracts from the plot and needs toning down.

Professional writers, after an initial panic, then a few days digesting the editor's call or letter, comply with these suggestions; they want to get their book published. And this is all before any contract is mentioned or signed.

Some writers refuse to change a word. The thought of doing any more work is enough to send them paranoid. But if you want to get your book published, then you will make these revisions to the best of your ability. You will make yourself do them. This is the attitude of a professional writer. If there is some aspect that really goes against the grain to change, then it's best to have a talk with the editor and see if some compromise can be reached.

While making editorial revisions, keep a list of page changes and briefly what has been rewritten. For example: 'Page 7 – more dialogue'. If the rewritten work creates an extra page, it's acceptable to number it '14A' or whatever it follows, without having to renumber the entire book. It helps the editor when she reads the revised MS if she can locate the new work immediately. She has probably read dozens of other books since looking at yours, and she'll appreciate a quick guide.

If an editor thinks that a marketable book can be made better, she'll enjoy working with a writer who listens, co-operates and can translate those suggestions into skilful writing. It could be the beginning of a good partnership.

10

THE LONG-DISTANCE WRITER

Writing is not a compartment of life, it is a whole existence. The solid truth about writing is if you don't write, then you are not a writer. Writers write and write every day if possible.

A day without writing is a lost day, never to be recovered; a day to mourn. Write something, anything – 1,000 words, 500, 100, your journal. Write when you first wake, any rambling phrases that come into your head. Let the thoughts flow down your arm and on to the paper. It feels good.

Sometimes this unconscious writing will gradually make sense. Sometimes lovely, out-of-context phrases appear. Keep them safe. They may come in useful when you least expect it.

Loneliness

The loneliness of the long-distance writer is undisputed. It is a solitary occupation, shut away in your ivory tower for hour after hour with only your thoughts and the green eye of your word processor.

Yet you are not truly alone because of all the people in your head and the ones you are creating on paper. They are your other world. The real loneliness comes from not being understood. Non-writers do not always understand what you need or what you are going through. They may not appreciate that you are desperate for time to yourself, peace and quiet, no trivial interruptions, but most important of all, that you need to be taken seriously. You are a writer.

So writers become isolated, wrapping themselves in a kind of thermal suit of armour to prevent the barbs of relationships and the community penetrating their vulnerability. They withdraw from a world that is often hostile to their profession.

Ernie Wise got it right when he protected his writer's fragile image with wild exaggeration: 'Yes, I wrote four plays this morning. Another five in the afternoon.'

How many times have you heard snide remarks like: 'You'll never finish it', 'It'll never get published', 'You're wasting your time', 'So you think you're a writer?', 'You want your head tested'?

So when my daughter (with kindness, though, in her heart) asks me what I've done today, instead of saying that I wrestled with two hopelessly inadequate pages, I'm far more likely to say: 'Wrote a book going up in the lift, two short stories over coffee, planned a saga while waiting for the bus.'

This turns my serious obsession into a joke, but allows me to get on with my writing.

For years I was a closet writer despite being published. I knew from experience that I lost friends if I told them that I wrote stories. A glassy look would steal into their eyes as if I had suddenly grown an extra ear; they stopped being natural and were wary of what they said in case they were being 'put into a book'.

How could I reassure them that I don't put real people into my books, that I have enough characters in my head for a hundred stories? Certainly a lot of facts are stored in my mental filing cabinet, but then they are stirred around with a spoonful of time and a pinch of imagination and re-appear in a totally different guise.

Now I don't tell anyone what I'm doing – except my writing friends. I joined the Romantic Novelists Association and the London Writers Circle; conferences and courses at Swanwick and Earnley were a revelation ... hearing first-class lectures, non-stop shop talk and making friends. For once people knew what you were talking about and wanted to listen and share experiences.

My advice is to keep your writing to yourself; shut yourself away and get on with it. Resist the temptation to chat around with friends. Save talking till you are with fellow writers.

For the rest of the year you can only accept the loneliness as being an occupational drawback, and be thankful that it is not the true loneliness of the recently widowed or the deserted wife or the forgotten hostage. There are people outside, waiting for you to rejoin the race.

Shortage of time

We are all short of time. Long-term time (life itself), short-term time (this week). It's the familiar wail of writers; some are genuine and some are using it as an excuse for not writing.

Excuses, excuses. Everything is an excuse.

'I've been too busy to write.' 'Hectic at the office.' 'Don't know where the time's gone.' What they really mean is that writing is not their first priority. I'm always hearing the feeblest excuses for not writing. If you really want to write, you'll find the time.

There is some period of time in every day if you look for it. And this applies if you work full-time or part-time at a bread-and-butter job as well as write. If you are a full-time writer, then planning and pacing your day is your main problem.

But for those who try to combine another occupation with writing, as well as running a household and bringing up children, time is as scarce as rain in the Sahara. It's easy to say get up earlier – 6 a.m. is a beautiful time of day when the world is fresh and quiet and you seem to have it all to yourself. I often do this if I'm nearing a deadline and this extra hour in the morning is beyond price.

I also work on the train, commuting to London, writing in longhand in a notebook, then type it on to a disc in the evening. This transfer is, in fact, its first revision. Weekends are earmarked for solid writing, morning, afternoon and evening, with time off only for a lightning strike at the shops and an early 9 a.m. swim at our leisure pool. I switch on my inner waterproof TV set and play out scenes of dialogue in my mind as I swim 32 lengths. That's half a mile. Keeping fit is another must.

Even the busiest mother should be able to find time for herself in the day, perhaps two separate half-hours when the children are napping. She should call this time her own and forget the ironing. I've typed with two toddlers sitting on my lap, both jamming the keys with sticky little fingers; now I'm more likely to have two big Persian cats on my lap with the four small fry reorganising my filing in a highly individual style.

You have to be ruthless, make time, be selfish. No one is going to say to you: 'Would you like this afternoon off for your writing, dear?'

Be professional in your attitude to your work; be seen to be serious in your determination to write and be published. Don't close the door on your family and then fritter the time writing letters or painting your nails. Save those activities for shared family time. When you are alone in your particular writing den/bedroom corner/under the stairs, use those precious hours to write and write.

Relationships

Juggling the roles of mother, wife, lover, husband, breadwinner with being a writer is a hard act to maintain. You keep dropping the balls. At some time you are going to get out of rhythm and find yourself facing a confrontation. Often the writing has to go to the wall.

A non-writing partner is going to find it difficult to accept that you enjoy shutting yourself away with all these imaginary people. He/she is likely to feel jealous, particularly if you are writing a romance and your hero is one dishy man and your heroine an absolute peach. Non-writers get aggrieved by the amount of time writers need to spend alone. They think that it reflects some kind of failure on their part.

Reassurance is the soothing ointment. Reassure your partner that these fictitious (use that word a lot) people, although very alive to you, are nothing like as good as the real thing. Sometimes a love scene you're writing can spill over into real life, which uses up a lot of calories.

Ask for help in the research, especially if you know nothing about cars or mechanical details. Include your partner in research trips even if you do lag behind with a notebook in your hand. Share your successes with the family. Celebrate with a meal out, a theatre trip, a holiday, depending on the size of your success. Share everything with them, except your writing time . . . and the storyline.

Don't tell your family the plot until it is in first draft. They can kill it off faster than a parliamentary guillotine with a few well-chosen words, and probably will. Keep the magic to yourself. Take care with your precise ideas. Talking about a story too early dissipates that magic. Why write it if you've already told everyone?

If your partner is also a writer, then I should imagine the problems are rather different, i.e. nobody makes the supper. But his-and-hers word processors could be fun . . . and talking way into the night . . . oh dear, that makes me feel quite weak, having a companion that compatible. Many writing partnerships seem to flourish, as long as they are not competing in the same field.

Children are easier to train, just remember to feed them regularly. They quite like having a mother/father who keeps out of their way and disappears for hours into the pantry with an ancient typewriter and a medieval thriller. Mine were born into a writing atmosphere. They have never known anything different. They know they can always interrupt me especially if they bring in a cup of tea. They spent their childhood charging down to the library to count how many times my books had been borrowed.

'Out forty-three times this year, Mum!'

God bless the Public Lending Right and all who work at the Registry.

Discipline

So there's a lack of time, a stroppy partner and nowhere to write; you could be forgiven for giving up. Self-discipline is your sword. You have got to make yourself write.

It would be so easy to forget the whole thing, switch on the telly and start knitting a sweater. No one needs to know that the cover hasn't been off your typewriter for weeks, dust welding the pages of your thesaurus. 'I'm no good, no good,' you weep into your third double Martini. But how do you know if you don't try and keep trying?

You need three firm disciplines:

- A definite start time
- A daily quota
- A realistic deadline

A definite start time

If you are at home all day, give yourself a morning starting time, like an office. Be at your desk promptly by 9.30 a.m. or 10 o'clock. On the dot. No excuses. Punch your card.

If you are a part-timer, then perhaps 8 p.m. is your time to clock in. Eight till eleven ... wonderful, three whole hours Three times five weekdays and that's fifteen hours. Two pages an hour (I'm slow) and that's thirty pages in a week ... 300 words a page and that's roughly 9,000 words. Keep this up for a month and a half and you've written a slim book.

Trollope set himself a daily number of words to write and kept a strict check on his output. It makes sense. I keep a daily record in a small Hallmark date book. Every working day I write down how many pages I write, revise or print. Any day off is recorded (sick/conference/research). Several blank days for no good reason will reproach me in neon lights and I am guilt-ridden.

A daily quota

Set yourself a realistic target each day. Two thousand words a day was too high for me and I couldn't reach it regularly. It made me feel a failure. Now my daily target is 1,000 (three to four pages) which I can reach and often exceed if the writing is going well. There is nothing wrong with a target as low as 500 or even less. It mounts up.

Two pages a day is a chapter in ten days ... another slim book in a hundred days. A daily quota is encouraging. It makes you work for it. But it's not a straitjacket ... it doesn't have to strangle you.

Another prolific writer has instead a weekly target of 15,000 words. Pretty high. But it does even out the good days and the bad days. She always takes the whole of Sunday off, or a different day if that's how it works out. She says she needs

one complete day to recuperate mentally and devote to her
family.

A realistic deadline

Impose a deadline for your work. Tell yourself that your
draft/revision/complete MS must be finished by Christmas/by
the date of your holiday/by the time the French children come
to stay. This kind of deadline sharpens the mind considerably.

If you have been commissioned to write a book, then you
will already have a contractual deadline which you should
strive to meet. Fingers crossed that you'll stay fit, find the
stamina and there are no family disasters.

If you don't meet your personal deadline, perhaps it was
unrealistic. You can't write an airport brick in slim-book time.
I set deadlines before some holiday or conference, so that I can
go off with a clear conscience and have a good time.

Somewhere to write

The kitchen table is not ideal. All that clearing away and
ketchup on the pages. But it's better than nothing. A book-lined
study with a panoramic penthouse view is beyond the hope of
most writers. I drool with envy over photographs of studies in
the Sunday supplements, long for endless shelves, acres of neat
desktop, everything in its place. My desk looks worked-on; it
has immense character somewhere beneath an Everest of paper.

Aim for a table or desk where you can leave out your work.
If you keep having to tidy away and then retrieve the MS from
a cupboard, you'll never get started. The sheer labour involved
will sap your strength.

Work in a nice room. A really nice room. Why should you

be banished like a nasty smell to share a cramped box room with broken tennis racquets or the far corner of a draughty, cheerless passage like an unwanted ghost? Perhaps a table could be installed in the dining room or the main bedroom with a bookcase for reference books and current files. Files stack flat on a bookshelf. Try to be organised so that it doesn't look like a municipal tip. Have a pottery jug for your pens, a pretty coaster for your coffee mug. People will start giving you things for your desk.

I work on a large dining table in the furthest corner of the dining room. There are two windows which look out on to the garden and a Japanese maple tree. Birds feed from the nut bags; cats stalk the birds, crouched on branches; sometimes it's hung with washing. The russet colour is warm and forever moving. It lives and breathes.

There are four bookcases at my side and two cork pin-boards on the wall for notes and pictures. The location means I am available for conversation (brief), the telephone (brief), making drinks (essential). Recently my box files and dozens of folders of research booklets and maps, stationery and carbon copies were moved upstairs to a tiny sewing room to cut down on the 'office' type clutter. So now I have an office upstairs and a writing desk downstairs. I am no longer surrounded by old research and cuttings that won't be looked at from one year's end to the other.

For some years I tried to write in this sewing room with half a desk propped against the sewing machine. It didn't work. The walls closed in on me. It was a prison. I like room to pace, to breathe freely with an acoustic curtain of music.

So the business side is now upstairs, out of the way, and I bring down what I want when I need it. One day I'll sort it all out. Meanwhile I'm writing in a tidier space.

Housework and shopping

Since this still seems to be mainly a female role despite all our attempts at equality, these remarks are addressed to women writers.

Better a dusty house than a dusty brain. Food, clothes, floors . . . those are the priorities. Feed everyone or encourage a rota system. (I'll cook supper tonight if you'll do it tomorrow, please?) Press all the right buttons for regular laundry sessions. Clean shirts, sheets, towels are essential. Wash and mop the kitchen floor. Keep housework to a hygenic minimum.

My vacuuming gets done at 11 p.m. A quick zip round to loosen stiff muscles and it's over for the day. I dust in snatches while my printer is at work. Two and a half minutes a page is a lot of dusting time. Polishing is reserved for when I'm upset; it's very therapeutic for frayed nerves.

Don't shop. Forget shops. More time is wasted wandering round the shops than anything else. We have to buy food and household necessities but know exactly what you are going out to buy. Time yourself, then cut down on that time. Walk faster.

Conferences, classes and writing courses

Conferences are invaluable. They stimulate and refill the well of ideas if it has run dry. A conference glowing keeps the writing flowing. There are so many being held now in all parts of the country. Look in *Writer's News* and *Writer's Monthly* for announcements.

Local creative-writing classes are a sensible opportunity for tuition for the beginner. Writing is a craft which can be learned and classes help you to avoid amateurish mistakes. Usually work is set weekly or ideas thrown at you. The one disadvantage is that the classes may be such fun that you never get round to start the book you really want to write. All your creative time is taken up by class work.

This also applies to correspondence courses. Some people find written criticism of their work very helpful, but that keeping up with a heavy course load leaves them with little time for any other writing.

There are so many excellent 'how-to' books available now that a library of them on your bookshelves may be all you need to get started.

Insomnia, illness and indolence

If you can't sleep, think up a story to amuse yourself. It may not be very good if you are fretting about another problem. It may be so good that you'll have to switch on the light and write it down.

Often when your brain is seething with plot and pushy characters, it's hard to make them go away and leave you alone to sleep. Writers need their sleep. Making bedtime into reading time can push these persistent people firmly back into their chapter while you enjoy someone else's book.

I always look forward to reading last thing at night. It's my reading time, my treat, my indulgence. It's surprising how many books you can get through in a year.

Illness comes to us all and writers quickly drain of physical and mental strength. Don't try to work if you are ill. Read instead. Surround yourself with a lovely pile of books and magazines, hot port for that sore throat, cats for company, read yourself into a healing sleep. When your hand reaches for a pen and jots down a phrase, you'll know you're getting better.

I wish indolence could be cured as simply. Indolence is a

personal trait. Only you know whether you are a lazy writer, that you talk more than you work. A writer is a person who writes and there are no other categories. If you don't write, then you are not a writer. You only think you are or wish you were. Wishful thinking won't get you published. No one can do anything about it except yourself. You have to generate that enthusiasm and will to work. If it's not there, be realistic and take up some other creative occupation.

Perhaps the genre is wrong for you. Why dream about a big novel when your soul sings poetry? Why struggle with an hour-long play if ideas for practical 500-word articles arrive in droves?

Indolence can be changed by hard work. It sounds a contradiction but pen to paper is the prescription. Small tasks of writing. Write ten separate words about how you are feeling or what you can see around you. Next day, write one sentence using one of those words. Feeling tired yet? On the following day write a short descriptive paragraph about a different word, and on the next day write another descriptive paragraph using a totally different viewpoint of the same word. These exercises stretch the mind and will make you feel less self-conscious about writing. Build up a writing habit.

If you still can't be bothered, then be honest, you are not really a writer.

Full-time, part-time, the hobby syndrome

I long to write full-time, to have a whole day for writing. It sounds bliss. Yet I'm told by one long-established author that she doesn't produce any more now that she has retired. The day vanishes. It is possible that one does not work quite so hard since there's the luxury of plenty of time.

Jonathan Gash (*Lovejoy*) says he will never give up his full-time job as a doctor and university lecturer. He would lose that frisson of excitement that he gets every evening when he sits down at his typewriter and knows it's his special time to work.

Part-time can be the best of both worlds despite the stress and tiredness and juggling. There's regular money coming in, and you have the stimulation of the outside world and the pleasure of your own writing time even if it's limited.

Writers have to eat; they can't live on ideas. So money nearly always has to be the deciding factor. Unless your book has been in the *Sunday Times* bestsellers list for 32 weeks, don't give up the day job. Very successful money-making authors do exist and we all long to join the ranks. But most writers could not live, to the same standard, on what they make solely from writing. Bread and diet bitter lemon in a garret might be some writer's dream of heaven, but I prefer central heating.

Beware of the hobby syndrome. Families in particular are prone to referring to 'Mum's little hobby'. It's a kind of put-down. Being serious about writing is not a hobby.

If you are published or aim to be published then you have entered the marketplace of profit and loss. Do not allow the word 'hobby' to be used in any way in relation to your writing. Stamp it out or be clever and make a joke out of it.

'Hobby? Oh yes, it's so rewarding and so lucrative. How else would I pay my library fines?'

Writing is work, my friends. Your way of life, your profession. Never forget it.

11

FIFTY WORDS EVERY WRITER NEEDS TO KNOW

Writers sometimes come up to me, bewilderment fixed on their faces, hesitation in every step. I almost know what they are going to say. 'Er, excuse me, but what is style?' 'What is back story?' 'This theme business . . . I thought I was writing a book.'

Like all crafts, writing has its trade words, and new writers don't know what they mean. For years I did not understand the difference between show and tell till Hugh C. Rae kindly explained it to me in words of one syllable, on the lawn at Swanwick between mouthfuls of home-made brown bread and blackcurrant jam.

So here is my instant glossary of fifty words every writer needs to know. Now you'll understand what everyone is talking about.

ACRONYM
Word formed from the initial letters of other words or syllables, i.e. AKA, WRAF, NATO.

ACTIVE VOICE
There are two ways of writing a statement, in the active voice or in the passive voice. The active voice is always more effective because it's simple and natural. For example:

They turned off the television.   ACTIVE.

The television was turned off.   PASSIVE
Jane made some tea.   ACTIVE.
The tea was made by Jane.   PASSIVE

Sometimes use of the passive voice is right, for example, 'the windscreen was shattered by a stone'. The windscreen has more importance than the stone in this sentence.

ADVANCE
This is the money paid to you by a publisher in advance of your own possible earnings. You do not have to return it if your book royalties don't reach that amount. New writers usually accept the suggested advance with gratitude; established bestsellers push it up.

AKA
A weird word coined by list-makers, abbreviating 'also known as' for when writers use more than one name, i.e. 'Stella Whitelaw aka Alexandra Thomas'.

ANTAGONIST
This is the character in opposition to your main characters, the trouble-maker, the catalyst; can be a person or a group of some kind.

BACKGROUND
This is the situation or setting where you choose to bring your characters to life, whether it be a hospital, a business, a particular country or city.

BACK STORY
This is what has happened to your characters before you begin your story. This is usually fed to the readers in small, digestible chunks.

BLURB

On the back of a book cover you'll find a few tantalising paragraphs written with the sole purpose of making you buy the book. This is known as the blurb. It's advertising material and is rarely written by the author.

CATEGORY ROMANCE

This is a small-sized paperback novel with a set number of pages (usually 186–188) and a set length of 50,000 to 55,000 words. 'A compact jewel' is how one American author describes this genre.

CLICHÉS

Clichés are words, expressions and situations which have become trite from overuse. There are a few acceptable ones but the rest should be avoided. Clichés come easily to mind when writing, but irritate the reader. They can be used in dialogue because it's our natural way of speaking. Most writers try to think of a different way of saying the same thing. Some clichés: pretty as a picture, long in the tooth, up with the lark, heart set on, lost for words.

There are cliché people too (the tart with a heart of gold, the eccentric professor, the grumbling cleaner) and cliché situations (the triangle, the misunderstanding, the overheard remark).

DEADLINE

The date by which your MS is due if you are contracted to a publisher. Be reliable. Your own personal deadline for work is an aid to disciplined writing.

EPONYM

This is a word coined from a person's name, i.e. sandwich, wellington, hoover.

FORMULA

Category romances have a basic happy-ending type plot. This is called a formula although the publishers stress that they want originality and fresh ideas, and the good writers manage to find them.

FBSR

First British Serial Rights are offered by the author when a short story or feature is sent to a magazine. This means that the magazine can publish the story/feature once only. It's not sensible to sell World Rights unless the editor insists. However, if you are a new writer, it'll make little difference if you let the World Rights go. Selling the Foreign Rights of published work is not easy unless you have an agent or know how to go about it.

FLASHBACK

A flashback is a scene from the past which is sometimes necessary to show a character's motivation or explain what happened previously. We are used to this device from television and films, but it should be used sparingly in a book. Readers get confused if you go backwards and forwards like a yo-yo.

GENRE

This refers to the types of popular fiction published, particularly romance, but there's also westerns, science fiction, spy stories, adventures, crime, whodunnits.

GLOSSIES

Expensive magazines printed on good-quality paper.

GOTHICS

Atmospheric stories, often centred around large gloomy houses with the heroine in great danger.

INTROSPECTION
A character's unspoken thoughts.

ISBN
The International Standard Book Numbering is what it says, a numbering system for all published books. Publishers get the ISBN from The Standard Book Numbering Agency Ltd, 12 Dyott Street, London, WC1A 1DF. It is not a legal requirement. There is no charge for numbering. No concern of author unless self-publishing.

METAPHOR
The comparison of one object to another by the transference of meaning, implying a resemblance. For example, 'He was a lion in battle'.

MINIMUM TERMS AGREEMENT
MTA champions a fair deal for authors. At least seven publishers have signed and their contracts are an immense improvement on the old chaos.

MIXED METAPHOR
Metaphors together which are incongruous, i.e. 'Without beating about the bush, he took off like a scalded cat.' And there's the politicans' favourite: 'With our shoulders to the wheel, we'll keep the flag flying.'

NARRATIVE
Relating events, telling a story as if you (the author) were that person, linking material between dialogue.

OUTLINE
This is a writer's visual and personal working guide, a practical

chapter-by-chapter breakdown of main scenes and events in the story and the development of the plot.

PACE
Pace carries the momentum of the plot. Long sentences slow things down. Short sentences add action, tension, suspense, immediacy. Stories need both.

PADDING
Unnecessary padding or waffle is overwriting. Too many words trying to say too little become boring and irrelevant. A padded book is a boring book. Cut, and cut again.

PARTIAL
Some publishers like to see a partial rather than the whole MS. A partial is usually the first two or three chapters with a synopsis, a brief covering letter and return postage.

PLOT
A plot is the story or plan of events arranged in sequence with a form of development. Plots usually come from the characters, but sometimes it's the other way round. Good plotting is planning a story ahead.

PLR
The Public Lending Right is the payment to authors from public funds, proportionate to the number of times that a book is lent out from selected libraries during the previous year. Authors have to register their titles and their ISBN with the PLR Office, Bayheath House, Prince Regent Street, Stockton-on-Tees, Cleveland, TS18 1DF. The last day for registering is the 30 June of each year. There is no charge.

PRINT RUN
This is the number of copies printed of a book.

PROOFS
Proofs are the printer's pages which the publisher sends to the author for correction. They are page by page, unbound, loose, on thin paper. Their purpose is for the author to correct mistakes, his and the printer's, not a last opportunity for re-writing. Every alteration costs money. There is an excellent list of proof-reading marks in the *Writers' and Artists' Year Book*.

PROTAGONIST
This is an ungainly word meaning the principal character in your story, usually the hero or heroine. It comes from the Greek, meaning the first actor.

PRUNING
Cutting with precision.

PULPS
Cheaper magazines printed on poor-quality paper.

READER IDENTIFICATION
The reader should be able to put him/herself in the shoes of the hero/heroine and understand their motivation, sympathise with them, live the story.

REMAINDER
A sad word meaning all the books left over when a publisher decides that a title has run out of steam. He sells them off, well below marked price, to cut-price bookshops and other writers rush to snap up the bargains.

ROYALTIES

This is the percentage of the retail price which the publisher agrees to pay you. It will be agreed in your contract. The average is ten per cent for hardbacks but it can be as low as two or three per cent on big sales of cheaper paperbacks. If it's based on net receipts, then the rate should be higher. The statements (and the cheque if sales have overtaken the advance) come twice a year.

SAGA

A long novel covering several generations or a period of years in a family. Very popular.

SEMANTICS

This is the study of the meaning of words. Fascinating. I wish I had the time.

SHORT FORMS

The short form of words used constantly: sd, wld, shd, abt, apx, tht. They save a lot of time when making notes or writing in longhand. Make up your own. I can't find a good one for 'the'.

SIMILE

The comparison of two unlike objects using 'like' or 'as' as joining words. For example: 'He ran like the wind', 'The lake was as still as glass', 'She was as sleepy as a cat'.

SLANT

To slant a story is when you write a story to meet the specific requirements of a magazine or publishing house.

'SHOW NOT TELL'

This is probably the hardest concept of writing to grasp, but simply means that a good writer shows what his characters are thinking and feeling, rather than telling the reader. There is a difference. Instead of making the plain statement that John is cold, let John show how cold he is by what he then says, does, or thinks.

For example: 'John was cold. He hated the snow.' Nothing really WRONG with this but we are being told.

' "I hate the snow," said John, shivering.' This is the BETTER way of showing.

Tell writing is straight reporting. Show writing is being and feeling.

STORYLINE

The storyline is the plot of a book, film, play; what happens next, then next again, the thread upon which everything hangs.

STYLE

Style is simply the individual way you write, the unique you, your voice, your tone, especially how you use words. The way you write sets the tone of the book and the reader will pick up on it, decide whether they like it and want to stay with the book. Your command of the English language, your choice of words, your interpretation of life is your style.

You may have several different styles: one for novels, one for short stories, or one for genre romances and a different, faster pace for thrillers.

There is little you can do to create style beyond the basic essentials of using simple language, cutting out long words, long sentences, clichés and overwritten prose.

Style is the essential you that will shine through your writing. It is as much part of you as your fingerprints or DNA. You can't copy another writer's style.

SYNOPSIS

Once more, a synopsis is a short, informative narrative covering the major content of a book, used to sell the work to an editor.

SYNTAX

This is about the construction of a sentence and the grammatical arrangement of words in a sentence. We unconsciously absorb this knowledge from reading well-written books.

TAG

This is a device giving a character some kind of personal label which sets him apart – a swagger, a loud laugh, a hat, a phrase. Watch characters in television series for ideas.

TEARSHEETS

These are the pages containing your story or feature that you tear out of a magazine. You may offer them to sell the foreign rights, send them as examples of your work if requested by an editor, or simply file them.

THEME

Most books have a theme even if you don't realise it. It's a statement about life and people, a universal truth that comes from the drama and conflict in the story. Love conquers all, faith works miracles, brothers under the skin (clichés) are obvious ones. This premise should be summed up in one sentence.

TIP SHEETS

Many publishers and magazines give away guidelines as to what kind of stories they are looking for. These are updated as lengths and requirements change.

TRANSITION

A sentence or two that moves the story on by linking scenes.

VANITY PUBLISHING

This is when an author pays a publisher for the production of his book. It is not to be recommended and is often very expensive. Never pay for publication unless you are a millionaire. If you are a millionaire with money to spare, why not start a new publishing company . . .?

VIEWPOINT

There are two viewpoints for telling your story. You can tell it in the first person, which is the single viewpoint, using the pronoun 'I' all the time. The third-person construction allows viewpoint from several different characters and 'he' and 'she' are used. Examples:

'I wandered along the seafront, feeling cold and depressed. It was the first time I had been on my own for years.' FIRST PERSON.

'She did not want to speak to him. She might say something she would regret.' THIRD PERSON.

A last word about viewpoint. Don't change viewpoint too often, and when you do so, make it clear.

VOICE

There is Active Voice and Passive Voice (see above) and also the Omniscient Voice of the author. This is the author talking like God, the all-seeing and all-knowing being. Sometimes it's known as the Narrative Voice, a different voice to that of first person or third person viewpoint.

WORD COUNT

A wise writer counts words. Most writers work out the average number of words per line (usually about ten to twelve) and the number of lines per page (usually 25, 26 or 27) and multiply. This would give an average of 250 or more words per page. Some word processors have a word count, but most publishers need to calculate white space as well. One word of dialogue on a line would still count as ten, and not one, because when it's printed it will take up a whole line.

WRITER'S BLOCK

This is not a guillotine for failed publishers. It describes the situation when a writer gets stuck, when an empty page or screen stares at them and they cannot think of a single word to write. A period of despair. (See Chapter 8.)

WRITER'S CRAMP

This is literally a muscular spasm, very painful, caused by prolonged writing. It can be caused by gripping a pen in a certain way or always hitting the space bar on a typewriter with ferocity. Your keyboard touch should be much lighter though it's hard for a former traditional typist to learn not to thump. Writer's cramp for keyboard users is more likely to appear in the form of backache or neck stiffness. Make sure your chair is the right height and your angle of viewing the screen is five degrees downwards. And move frequently. Get up and walk about. Stretch. Make coffee. Look out of the window.

That's more than fifty words, but who's going to waste time counting them? It's the moment to start work again. There's that image of an owl caught in my headlights as it washes itself in a puddle . . . I can still see the shower of raindrops flying everywhere as he shook out his speckled wings, his big eyes glowing and totally unafraid. I can't wait to start writing . . .